Practical Life Application
From a Biblical Perspective

Practical Proverbs™

Bible Study and Life Management
Course for the Younger Student

By Dara Halydier

www.practicalproverbs.com

Practical Proverbs

ISBN # 978-0-615-57674-9

Published by:
TD Publishing
PO Box 3102
Early, TX 76803
Printed in the United States of America

About the Author:

Dara Halydier is a daughter of the King. She is a mother of five boys who are continuing their journeys in faith and ministry across the United States. Dara has homeschooled for 21 years. Dara is married to a wonderful, supportive husband, Tracy. They currently reside in Central Texas. Dara has been a speaker for retreats and conferences in several states and enjoys teaching Bible studies in her local area.

You can view Dara's website at www.abidingtruthministry.com or contact her at Dara@abidingtruthministry.com.

Instructions for Practical Proverbs

Practical Proverbs for Younger Students is geared towards your 4th through 8th grade and up student however some 3rd graders might be ready for this more in depth study and some high school students will gain from these basic truths. The author suggests that 3rd-6th graders go through this study with a parent. 7th-8th graders could do the work on their own, but it is suggested that the parent be involved to answer any questions that the students might have beyond the written content. If your high school student has not thought through and sought God's Word about some of these topics, they will benefit from this book as well.

This book is not an expositional study of Proverbs like our Practical Proverbs for Older Students. This book will give your child some background in the history of Israel, King David, Solomon, and the kingdom split under King Rehoboam. The topics are all found in Proverbs and the author tried to include as much of Proverbs as she could. Other Old and New Testament verses are included as well as the grace and mercy given to us through Jesus Christ. **The author chose to use the New American Standard Bible.** It will be easier for your student if they have a copy of this version available.

This study includes 36 lessons on 36 topics. After each lesson is a worksheet - a few lessons have two worksheets. The teacher/student can go through the lesson and worksheet in one sitting, or they can go through the lesson and assign the worksheet as homework, or they can do the lesson one day and do the worksheet the next day as a separate lesson. The worksheets were designed to make each topic applicable to the student's life. All answers are available in the answer key book.

Bible memory exercises are found at the end of each lesson. If your student already has these verses memorized, feel free to assign a different verse.

There is also a list of recommended books in Appendix A. As the teacher, you decide if these books are appropriate and timely in your student's life and assign them as you see fit. As a parent of a pre-teen or teen you might want to read some of the recommended reading yourself to be better prepared for the next stage of your child's life.

May your study of the Scriptures be blessed,
Dara Halydier

Practical Proverbs

Table of Contents

Practical Proverbs

Introduction

What is wisdom? There is the wisdom of the ages, Biblical wisdom, wise sayings, wise cracks, and wise guys. But where do we find true wisdom? Is there a universal, absolute wisdom? Is wisdom knowledge? Understanding? Application? Or maybe all three?

Wisdom has to do with choices: On what to base our choices, weighing our choices, and understanding the consequences of our choices. Choices about life, relationships, money, religion, duties, and even what to wear or eat and when, with whom, and how long.

Proverbs is a book of wisdom written by Solomon, the wisest man that ever lived according to God. Proverbs is a great place to start our treasure hunt as we search for nuggets of wisdom. Along the way we will learn about ourselves, our friends, our families, and our God.

To understand wisdom, we must also look at its opposite: foolishness. What are the characteristics and results of foolish choices? Of wise choices? Do my choices impact only me and my immediate situation? Or could a bad choice haunt me for a very long time?

My prayer for you is that you will gain not only knowledge about wisdom, but that you will gain wisdom on how to apply wisdom to your life. I pray that you may desire God's choices for each decision that will come up in your future and that you will grow closer to God who loves you and has a plan and a purpose for your life.

What is Wisdom?

Lesson 1

The proverbs of Solomon, the son of David,
king of Israel; To know wisdom and instruction,
To discern the saying of understanding...
Proverbs 1:1-2

Draw a picture of a cat.

Cover up your picture and have your Mom or Dad or a sibling or friend draw a picture of a cat.

Practical Proverbs

Do they look alike? ______ Are they the same type of cat? ______

Are they the same color? ______ Are they doing the same thing? ______

All of us have different ideas of the same word "cat". If we are cat lovers we might draw a heart around our picture, whereas if we are dog lovers, we might have a dog chasing the cat!

This is true of other words, too. So let's make sure we are using the same definitions for some key words.

What does the word "God" mean to you? ________________________________
____

When I talk about "God", I am talking about the God of creation that tells us about Himself in the Bible.

Another word that we will be using is "wisdom".

Who do you know who is wise?____

Why do you think that this person is wise? _____________________________

Circle the words or phrases that you think of when you think of wisdom:

Intelligent   Old   Experienced   Know lots about a lot

Good at counseling others   Knows a lot of Bible verses   Has good judgment

Chooses the same kinds of things that I like

The American Heritage Dictionary of the English Language says that wisdom is: "Understanding what is true, right, or lasting," or "Common sense and good judgment."

In your world what is true? ______________________________________

What do you think is right? ______________________________________

What will last? ____

Look up these verses and they will help you answer the next few questions wisely!

Isaiah 40:8
Psalm 119:160
John 14:6
Psalm 19:8

According to these verses where are we going to find wisdom? _______________

Read James 1:5. How can we obtain wisdom? _____________________________

Take a minute and pray to God and ask Him to give you wisdom as you go through this course to hear His Word and to apply it to your life.

We will be memorizing a definition for wisdom and using it throughout this book. So go ahead and start memorizing!

Wisdom is the ability to judge correctly and use our knowledge to avoid trouble, solve problems, reach goals, and succeed in life based upon God's principles.

Here is a crossword puzzle for you to do. You will find the answers in Proverbs chapter 8. These clues were taken from the New American Standard Bible. If you use a different Bible it will be necessary for you to really think through the sentences and consider words that will fit into the puzzle. If there is an "a" after the chapter and verse, it means that the clue will be found in the first part of the verse. A "b" means the clue will be found in the second half of the verse.

Down

1. 8:17b "And those who ____________________ seek me will find me."
2. 8:14b "I am ______________________."
3. 8:18b "Enduring ________________________ and righteousness."
4. 8:10b "And ____________________ rather than choicest gold."
5. 8:20a "I walk in the way of righteousness, in the midst of the paths of ______________."
10. 8:9b "And _________________ to those who find knowledge."
12. 8:14c "_________________ is mine."
13. 8:30b "And I was daily His ______________________."
15. 8:8a "All the utterances of my mouth are in _______________________________."
18. 8:35 "He who finds me finds __________________________."

Across

6. 8:10a "Take my ____________________ and not silver."
7. 8:14a "_________________ is mine and sound wisdom."
8. 8:7a "For my mouth will utter _________________."
9. 8:32a "For _____________________ are they who keep my ways."
11. 8:18a "Riches and _______________ are with me."
12. 8:12a "I, wisdom, dwell with ______________________."
14. 8:9a "They are all ________________________ to him who understands."
16. 8:19a "My fruit is better than __________________."
17. 8:13a "The fear of the Lord is to ___________ ___________."
19. 8:17a "I love those who ___________________ me."

1
2
3
4
5
6
7
8
9
10
11
12
13
14
15
16
17
18
19

Wisdom vs. Knowledge

Lesson 2

To receive instruction in wise behavior,
Righteousness, justice and equity;
To give prudence to the naïve,
To the youth knowledge and discretion.
Proverbs 1:3-4

Now that you know what wisdom is you need to understand the difference between wisdom and knowledge. Can you have one without the other? Which comes first? Let's find out!

Knowledge is having the facts about something.

How is this different from wisdom? ____

Take this quick quiz and see if you can figure it out.

1. Being able to identify all the constellations
   a. Wisdom
   b. Knowledge
   c. Both

2. Being able to read a manual and complete a project
   a. Wisdom
   b. Knowledge
   c. Both

3. Being able to decipher a graph and tell others about it
   a. Wisdom
   b. Knowledge
   c. Both

4. Being able to decide whether to smoke or not
   a. Wisdom
   b. Knowledge
   c. Both

5. Being able to discover whether or not someone should be your friend
   a. Wisdom
   b. Knowledge
   c. Both

You should have answered that numbers 1, 2, and 3 take knowledge; but be careful! Numbers 4 and 5 take knowledge and wisdom; don't they?

That's right. **Knowledge comes before wisdom**. We must gather some facts in order to make a wise decision.

Where does understanding fit into this? Just because I know that the cosine of 60 is 0.95241298, does not mean that I understand what a cosine is or how to do the math to figure it out. I need to know and understand something before I can wisely use the information to make a decision.

What do you think that we should know and understand in order to be wise?

____

Jesus speaks to his disciples in Luke 24:44-45.

"Now He said to them, 'These are My words which I spoke to you while I was still with you, that all things which are written about Me in the Law of Moses and the Prophets and the Psalms must be fulfilled.' Then he opened their minds to ______________________ the Scriptures."

According to these verses, what did Jesus want the disciples to understand?

____

That's right!! Jesus wants his disciples to understand the Scriptures - the Bible. Before we can understand the Scriptures, we have to know the Scriptures. We do that by reading the Bible and memorizing Bible verses and passages.

How much Bible do you know?

a. A little
b. Some
c. Quite a bit
d. Lots

Do you understand all that you know? ___________

If you think that you understand all that you know then explain to me how God spoke the world into being!! There are some things in the Bible that we can know but not really understand. But that's okay, because God understands it all and He will reveal Himself to us little by little. For now, just be faithful in reading and knowing the Bible. God will help you understand it as you grow.

Practical Proverbs 

Now would be a good time for you to decide to read the Bible every day. **Sign your name below if you are willing to make that commitment.** (An occasional sick or sleep in day may happen, but try as best you possibly can to do it every day.)

____

Keep working on memorizing your definition of wisdom. Fill in these blanks and see how you do.

Wisdom is the ability to _____________ correctly and use our _______________ to avoid ___________, solve ______________, reach ____________, and succeed in life based upon __________ principles.

So faith comes by hearing,
and hearing by the word of Christ.
Romans 10:17

Knowledge comes from hearing (or reading) God's Word. Colossians 3:16 urges us to ***"Let the word of Christ richly dwell within you…"***

Read Hebrews 5:11-14. What is God's word compared to? ___________________

That's right it is food: either milk or solid food. Which one are you ready for? ___________
If you are a new Christian it is okay to need milk, but if you have been a Christian for some time, then you should have matured to be able to read and understand the meatier things of the Word of God.

How many days of the week do you eat real food such as meat and vegetables?
____

How many days of the week do you think you should eat the spiritual food of the Bible? ____________________

If you eat of God's Word daily and spend time with Jesus then you will grow healthy spiritually.

Draw a line from each verse to the food or drink that it mentions.

Galatians 5:22
1 Peter 2:2
John 6:35
1 Corinthians 10:1-4
1 Corinthians 3:1-2 (KJV says "meat" instead of "food")

If you do not read God's word daily, now that you know how important it is, plan to make time every day to read and pray. If you don't know where to start, try Genesis or Matthew.

Definitions

Lesson 3

A wise man will hear and increase in learning,
And a man of understanding will acquire wise council...
Proverbs 1:5

Read Proverbs 1:1-4

These verses tell us why Solomon wrote the book of Proverbs. But before we look at that, check out verse 8 and see who he wrote it for. That's right! Proverbs is a love letter from a father to his son. It was written from someone who had been there; done that. Solomon made plenty of mistakes (more on him in lesson 5) and he wanted to help his son avoid making the same mistakes. Unfortunately, Rehoboam, one of his sons, didn't listen, and when he became king he really messed up and the kingdom of Israel was divided into two nations: Israel and Judah with Rehoboam only getting two of the ten tribes to rule over.

Do you always listen to your Mom or Dad? _______________

Write about a time when you didn't listen and it landed you in trouble.

Okay, back to verses 1-4. There are a few words here that we should be sure to define and explain. For each word write out what you think it means before looking into a dictionary. Then write out a dictionary definition. Lastly, look at what we are going to call our "working definition".

1. Wisdom

   Your definition:

   The dictionary definition:

   Our working definition: **The ability to judge correctly and use our knowledge to avoid trouble, solve problems, reach goals, and succeed in life based upon God's principles.**

2. Knowledge
   Your definition:

   The dictionary definition:

   Our working definition: **Having the facts**

3. Instruction
   Your definition:

   The dictionary definition:

   Our working definition: **Putting information in order; preparing, teaching, arranging, and building up information so it can be utilized.**

4. Discernment
   Your definition:

   The dictionary definition:

   Our working definition: **Being able to distinguish between good and evil, leading us to act with wisdom.**

5. Prudence
   Your definition:

   The dictionary definition:

   Our working definition: **Being wise in handling practical matters, careful about one's conduct.**

6. Naïve
   Your definition:

   The dictionary definition:

   Our working definition: **Having no knowledge**

7. Discretion
   Your definition:

   The dictionary definition:

   Our working definition: **Thinking about and applying wisdom before it comes out in words or actions.**

Practical Proverbs

Using our working definitions tell in your own words why Solomon wrote the book of Proverbs. Use Proverbs 1:1-4 as a guide.

Now look at verses 5 and 7 and fill in these blanks.

5 A _________________ man will hear and increase in learning, and a man of ___________________________ will acquire wise counsel…

7 The fear of the Lord is the beginning of knowledge; _____________ despise wisdom and instruction.

Which will you choose to be: a wise man or a fool? _______________________

Good job! You are gaining knowledge!

Keep working to memorize the working definition of wisdom.

Wisdom is the ability to _____________ correctly and use our _______________ to avoid ___________, solve______________, reach ____________, and succeed in __________ based upon __________ principles.

Counsel is mine and sound wisdom;
I am understanding; power is mine.
Proverbs 8:14

Words of Wisdom

Wisdom	Prudence	Wise Behavior
Knowledge	Naïve	Wise Counsel
Instruction	Discretion	Proverb
Discernment	Understanding	Righteousness

K	W	I	S	E	C	O	U	N	S	E	L	R
W	N	T	I	N	S	G	N	A	W	P	P	I
I	R	N	B	W	S	N	R	M	I	R	R	G
S	P	E	A	C	E	I	O	K	N	O	U	T
E	R	M	V	K	N	D	S	N	O	V	D	H
B	O	N	T	M	S	N	C	O	I	E	E	E
E	B	R	L	I	U	A	V	U	T	R	N	G
H	P	E	W	J	O	T	T	N	E	B	C	D
A	R	C	S	U	E	S	L	D	R	M	E	E
V	U	S	H	R	T	R	E	S	C	S	P	L
I	T	I	N	G	H	E	T	V	S	N	S	W
O	L	D	E	O	G	D	A	N	I	I	R	O
R	M	D	T	P	I	N	V	W	D	A	O	N
W	I	N	S	T	R	U	C	T	I	O	N	K

I, Wisdom, dwell with prudence,
And I find knowledge and discretion.
Proverbs 8:12

WORD BANK

Wisdom | Instruction | Discernment | Discretion
Knowledge | Prudence | Naïvity

Use the words form the word bank above to answer what you would need in each situation. You may use each word more than once or not at all.

1. Your cell phone fell into a mud puddle. You are feeling very naïve about how to fix it.
   What do you need? ____________________

2. You found out that you can put the phone in the oven to dry it out.
   Now what do you need so that you don't burn it? ____________________

3. You see two people fighting.
   What do you need? ____________________

4. You saw the answer key to this page. Should you cheat?
   What do you need? ____________________

5. You are going to the pool with a group of boys and girls, and you are trying to decide whether you should wear a t-shirt over your swimsuit.
   What do you need? ____________________

6. Your dad bought your mom a birthday present and you know what it is. She asks you to give her a hint.
   What do you need? (Besides self-control!) ____________________

7. You know that you should use a particular formula to solve a math problem, but you are not sure how to use it.
   What do you need? ____________________

8. You are praying about what you ought to be when you grow up.
   What do you need? ____________________

9. You are really angry over what your friend said to you.
   What do you need? ____________________

10. You are having a hard time thinking good thoughts about yourself.
    What do you need? ____________________

Fear of the Lord

Lesson 4

The beginning of wisdom is: Acquire wisdom;
And with all your acquiring, get understanding.
Proverbs 4:7

You read yesterday that the, ***"Fear of the Lord is the beginning of knowledge."*** (Proverbs 1:7). So what does the fear of the Lord mean and what does it have to do with knowledge and wisdom?

The fear of the Lord comes when we acknowledge our sin and seek God. The more we know Him, the more we fear Him because He is just, holy, righteous, and perfect, and He holds our future in His hands. Now, if we are without sin, then we do not need to fear God.

Think of it this way. You just robbed a bank. You are running away from the crime scene and you see a policeman. You are afraid of him because you know that he could put you away in prison for a long time. You understand that he is your judge and you fear his capturing you. But if you are out on a picnic with your family and you have committed no crimes and you see a policeman you might walk right up to him and say "Hi." The Bible talks about this in the book of Romans. Read Romans 13:3-4.

And we have all sinned against this perfect, holy God. As we begin to understand God as our Creator, as Judge, as Lord over all the earth, we will fear Him because we are guilty (before accepting Jesus as Lord and Savior).

Write out Romans 3:23 below.

____

____

In archery "sin" is missing the bull's eye or missing the mark. So anything that we have ever done that missed the mark of God's perfection is sin. Yep, welcome to the human race – **all have sinned.** That is what made Jesus so special, He never sinned!! But He was not just human, He was also God!

Having the knowledge that we have sinned should make us fearful of the Creator God who will judge.

But!!!

God loved us so much, that He couldn't stand to judge us, so He sent His perfect Son to come to earth and take our judgment of death for us! All we have to do is accept it!

Read Romans 6:23. What are the wages of sin? ____________________________

Practical Proverbs

You've sinned, you deserve death. But God gave us a gift of eternal life by believing in His Son, Jesus.

If you have never asked Jesus to forgive you of your sins and to come and lead you through this life, then bow your head now and tell Him that you are sorry and want a relationship with Him and eternal life. If you are not quite sure, ask your Mom and Dad, or an adult at your church what all of this means.

If you feared God's judgment and prayed for forgiveness then **knowledge of your sins and of God's gift of grace is the beginning of wisdom in your life**. Remember that **wisdom is about seeing and doing life God's way!** Now you never have to fear God again. You can go right up to Him with confidence and say, "Hi!"

Fill in these blanks from Colossians 2:2-3.

"…that their hearts may be encouraged, having been knit together in love, and attaining to all the wealth that comes from the full assurance of ______________________, resulting in a true ___________________ of God's mystery, that is Christ Himself, in whom are hidden all the treasures of ______________________ and ________________________."

You are on your way!!

Read Colossians 2:13-14.

What did God forgive you for? ______________________________________ (That's another word for sins).

You are no longer dead but ____________________ together with Him (Now and for all eternity!)

What did God cancel? ____ (That's what we owed Him for our sins.)

Where did God nail that statement of judgment against us? ________________ (That's right – the cross of Jesus!)

Now we don't owe God anything and we can go to Him with confidence and assurance and joy and love and ask Him for wisdom about everything!! What a great God!!

We are going to be memorizing some verses in Proverbs. **Start memorizing Proverbs 3:5-6**. To help you, fill in the blanks on the next page.

3:5 "Trust in the _______________ with all your _______________
And do not lean on your own___________________________.

3:6 In all your ways ______________________ Him,
And He will make your paths______________________.

CHALLENGE: If you already have these two verses memorized, start at verse 1 and memorize through verse 6.

Your wisdom definition is to be completely memorized before you start lesson 5!!

Wisdom is the _____________ to _______________ _______________ and use our ______________________ to _____________trouble, ___________ problems, ____________ goals, and _____________ _____ __________ based upon God's principles.

The fear of the Lord is the beginning of wisdom;
A good understanding have all those who do His commandments;
His praise endures forever. Psalm 111:10

As a Christian do you need to fear the final judgment of God which is also called the Great White Throne Judgment? No!! You have been judged and found innocent by Jesus' blood. Romans 8:1 should give you confidence. "***There is now therefore no _________________ for those who are in Christ Jesus.***" However, God *is* going to hand out crowns at the judgment. Look up these verses and see what crowns you could receive.

Match the crown to its reason by drawing lines.

To those who with patience endured trials (James 1:12)

To those who are faithful in ministering the word (1 Peter 5:1-4)

To those who love Jesus' appearing (2 Timothy 4:8)

To those who live a disciplined life (1 Corinthians 9:25)

To those who joyously expressed their faith (1 Thessalonians 2:19-20)

Like Father, Like Son

Lesson 5

How blessed is the man who finds wisdom
And the man who gains understanding.
Proverbs 3:13

Before we get started on today's lesson, **recite your wisdom definition to your teacher**.

You can do this lesson as a reading or as a play. You will need 6 voices. You can find 5 people to do it with you or you can each do more than one voice.

The place: The nation of Israel in the King's palace in Jerusalem
The date: 970 B.C.
Characters: David – King of Israel, old and frail
Bathsheba – Queen of Israel
Nathan – Prophet of God
Benaiah – Priest of Israel
God – Yahweh, Creator God
Solomon – Son of David and heir to the throne of Israel
Setting: King David is lying on his bed. He is an old man, sick and shaking. The window curtains are drawn and it is night. Nearby is his nurse, Abishag. She is busy and trying not to look too interested in what is going on at the bedside. A guard stands at attention next to the door. (Taken from 1 Kings 1-2)

Scene I

(As the curtain rises Nathan the prophet comes into the room, bows, and addresses King David.)

Nathan: "My lord the king, have you said, 'Adonijah, my son, shall be king after me, and he shall sit on my throne'?"

David: "Call Bathsheba to me."
(Bathsheba comes in bowing before the king and stands next to the bed, Nathan steps back into the background.)

David: "As the Lord lives, who has redeemed my life from all distress, surely I vowed to you by the Lord the God of Israel, saying, 'Your son Solomon shall be king after me, and he shall sit on my throne in my place'; I will indeed do so this day."

Bathsheba: (bowing her face to the ground before the king) "May my lord King David live forever."

David: (To a guard) "Call to me Zadok the priest, Nathan the prophet, and Benaiah the son of Jehoida." (Guard exits.)

Curtain closes

Scene II

(Curtain opens on same scene. Abishag is gone and so is the guard. Nathan and Benaiah are standing next to the king's bed.)

David: "Take with you the servants of your lord, and have my son Solomon ride on my own mule, and bring him down to Gihon. Let Zadok the priest and Nathan the prophet anoint him there as king over Israel, and blow the trumpet and say, 'Long live King Solomon!' Then you shall come up after him and he shall come and sit on my throne and be king in my place; for I have appointed him to be ruler over Israel and Judah."

Benaiah: "Amen! Thus may the Lord, the God of my lord the king, say."

Curtain closes

Scene III

(Curtain opens on same scene, but windows are open and it is daylight. Solomon with the crown upon his head bows beside his father's bed.)

David: "I am going the way of all the earth. Be strong, therefore, and show yourself a man. Keep the charge of the Lord your God, to walk in His ways, to keep His statutes, His commandments, his ordinances, and His testimonies, according to what is written in the Law of Moses, that you may succeed in all that you do and wherever you turn, so that the Lord may carry out His promise which He spoke concerning me, saying, 'If your sons are careful of their way, to walk before Me in truth with all their heart and with all their soul, you shall not lack a man on the throne of Israel.'"

Curtain closes

Scene IV

(Curtain opens. All is dark. Spotlight shines on King Solomon kneeling on the ground in prayer.)

God: (Voice from off stage) "Ask what you wish me to give you."

Solomon: "You have shown great lovingkindness to Your servant David my father, according as he walked before You in truth and righteousness and uprightness of heart toward You; and You have reserved for him this great lovingkindness, that You have given him a son to sit on his throne, as it is this day. Now, O Lord, my God, You have made Your servant king in place of my father David, yet I am but a little child; I do not know how to go out or come in. Your servant is in the midst of Your people which You have chosen, a great people who are too many to be numbered or counted. So give Your servant an understanding heart to judge Your people to discern between good and evil. For who is able to judge this great people of Yours?"

God: "Because you have asked this thing and have not asked for yourself long life, nor have you asked riches for yourself, nor have you asked for the life of your enemies, but have asked for yourself discernment to understand justice, behold, I have done according to your words. Behold, I have given you a wise and discerning heart, so that there has been no one like you before you, nor shall one like you arise after you. I have also given you what you have not asked, both riches and honor, so that there will not be any among the kings like you all your days. If you walk in My ways, keeping My statues and commandments, as your father, David, walked, then I will prolong your days."

(Light fades to black. Curtain closes)

END OF PLAY

Let's review a few things. David was a good king, but he was also human and thus a sinner. He wanted to marry a girl named Bathsheba and they sinned, but since she was already married to another man, David had her husband killed so that he could marry her. So, why did God still honor David? **REPENTENCE!** David knew he had blown it. He wrote several Psalms or songs about it. (See Psalm 51) He was sorry for what he had done! He asked God's forgiveness and he was forgiven. Later, after David married Bathsheba she gave birth to Solomon. Even though Solomon was not the oldest of David's sons, David still promised him the kingdom!

Solomon was the greatest king of Israel. He was richer, smarter, had more peace with the neighboring countries, and ruled over the largest land mass and more people of any other king of Israel before or after him. But, he, too, was not perfect and he sinned. Remember God telling him to walk in God's ways? Well, he did some of the time, but Solomon married more than one girl even though God had forbidden the kings of Israel to have more than one wife. These wives led King Solomon away from God and he worshipped other false gods and idols. He was the wisest man ever, and yet, he **chose** to do what he wanted, not what God had commanded.

Practical Proverbs 

Solomon's story ends well, though. After trying everything that the world had to offer: wealth, ambition, wives, horses, etc…, he turned back to God. Listen to the closing words of his book, Ecclesiastes: ***"The conclusion, when all has been heard, is: fear God and keep His commandments, because this applies to every person. For God will bring every act to judgment, everything which is hidden, whether it is good or evil."***

Write the working definition of wisdom here:

Wisdom is ____
____
____
____

Will you choose knowledge alone, or knowledge and wisdom?________________

Keep working on memorizing Proverbs 3:5-6.

3:5 "Trust in the ________________ with all your ________________
And do not ________ on your own____________________________.
3:6 In all your ____________ ________________________ Him,
And He will make your _____________ ________________________."

The sacrifices of God are a broken spirit;
A broken and a contrite heart, O God, You will not despise.
Psalm 51:17

Psalm 51 was the Psalm that David wrote when repenting of his sin of taking Bathsheba for his wife and killing her husband. Let's take a close look at David's heart through Psalm 51. **Read each verse as you go through this sheet.**

Praise to God

Verses 1-2 David acknowledges who God is and what He is able and willing to do. God is gracious, loving, kind, compassionate, and able to make the sinner clean and willing to do so.

Confession

Verses 3-4 David acknowledges his sin, whom he sinned against, and God's right to judge him based on God's character of being blameless.

Praise for Jesus

Verses 5-6 David acknowledges his own sin nature (it is not a sin for a mom and dad to conceive a child, but we are all born with a sin nature) and God's desire that David know truth and wisdom. Remember that in the New Testament truth and wisdom *is* Jesus Himself! That is the only cure for the sin nature. We must be born again.

Spending Time with God

Verses 7-9 David again, is pleading to God to make him clean. Nothing else will do. And only after being cleansed will David again know joy and gladness. **Joy is always linked to the presence of God in Scripture.** David is asking God to not only forgive him, but to forget his sins. Verse 8 is speaking of broken bones – that is a picture of a shepherd, who when he has a young sheep that insists on wandering off into danger, will break the leg of the sheep and carry it close to his heart until it is healed. During this recovery, the sheep learns to love and listen to the Shepherd. God sometimes must "break a bone" to get us to listen. That broken bone may be an illness or something else that comes into our lives that makes us be still and listen to God.

Confession

Verse 10-12 David knows that **a clean heart and a steadfast spirit come only from God**. David is begging for fellowship with God.

Intercession

Verse 13 David is vowing to use his life to teach these truths to others that they might be converted to God. Intercession is praying for others, but also asking God how He wants to use us that others may know Him.

Praise

Verse 14-15 David is referring to the blood sacrifices required in the Old Testament for atonement of sins. Romans and Hebrews in the New Testament remind us that we no longer have to make these sacrifices because Jesus shed His blood once for all. The result of being declared righteous through the blood sacrifice leads him to praise.

Introspection

Verses 16-17 These verses give us a glimpse into God's heart. Yes, God set up the old laws of sacrifice, but they were just a foreshadowing of what we would have in Jesus, and once Jesus came we no longer have to sacrifice animals, but we need to have a broken and contrite heart before God, **thus a loving desire to be with Him and praise Him based not on acts, but on love.**

Acknowledge God as Lord

Verses 18-19 David ends with a prayer for Zion - Jerusalem. When Jerusalem is protected physically and spiritually, then the sacrifices would be acceptable, because they would not come from duty, but from hearts of love.

Write your own prayer. Use the headings below and put your thoughts into a prayer

Praise to God (Who God is)

Confession

Praise for Jesus

Spend time with God

Intercession (for others)

Praise

Introspection (Is my heart right with God and what does God want me to do)

Acknowledge God as Lord over all

Who is Wisdom?

Lesson 6

Acquire wisdom! Acquire understanding!
Do not forget nor turn away from the words of my mouth.
Do not forsake her, and she will guard you;
Love her, and she will watch over you.
Proverbs 4:5-6

So, we know that we should work to get wisdom, but how! What is wisdom? I think you will be surprised at the answer as we figure out this riddle.

Turn to Proverbs 8. Think of wisdom as a person. Read verses 22-31.

Who was with God from the beginning? ______________________________

To see if you are right, **turn to John 1:1-5 and 1:9-14**.

That's right! Jesus was with God from the beginning. He was the Master Workman and He delights in the sons of man; so much so, that He was willing to come and live among them and die for them!

Now that you know that Wisdom is Jesus, **go back through all of Proverbs 8** and put the name of Jesus in for each time that you read "wisdom" or "her" referring to wisdom.

What new characteristics did you find out about Jesus?

____

____

I especially love verse 17: ***"...and those who diligently seek Me will find me."***

Look at verses 32, 7, and 35 and fill in the blanks for John 14:6.

"_____________________ said to him, "I am the _________________, the _______________, and the ____________ ; no one comes to the Father but through me."

So...if you want wisdom, you have to first have Jesus and if you have Jesus, you have wisdom.

But, if you have Jesus you can still act foolishly if you don't find out about Him, talk to Him, and listen to Him!!

Fill in the blank for this verse found in James 1:5.
"But if any of you lacks ______________________, let him _____________ of God, who gives to all generously and without reproach, and it will be given to him."

So, who is the source of wisdom? ______________________________
Does He want to keep it all to Himself? __________________________
What do you have to do to get this wisdom? ______________________

The next verse, James 1:6, gives us further direction.

"But, he must ask in ________________ without any doubting, for the one who doubts is like the surf of the sea, driven and tossed by the wind."

According to this verse, what is the opposite of faith? _______________________

That's right, doubt. **Faith is believing that God is who He says He is and that He will do what He says He will do!** Doubt is unbelief. Just remember that God's answer is not always "Yes." Sometimes, it is "No," or "Wait awhile." But always remember that God loves you, knows what is best for you, and will answer your prayers. God never promises the Christian that life will be easy and stress free. He does promise to be there with us through it all – pain, suffering, grief, etc.

When people started reading the Bible again after the many years during the Dark Ages, or Medieval Ages, they suffered for believing God's Word. Many gave up their lives like the early church did. Many slaves here in America were believers, but suffered great atrocities. There are more Christians being martyred for their faith in the 21st century than ever before in history. Does God not love them? Does He not care? Does He not answer their prayers?

God does hear and answer their prayers and gives them grace and mercy and wisdom in the midst of their pain. He gives them the knowledge that suffering here on earth will only last a minute, but blessings of eternal life are forever!!

Read 2 Corinthians 4:17-18. Should we be looking at the things that happen to us here on earth or looking forward to the reward of heaven? ____________________

Don't lose heart. God has a plan. He wins in the end and I want to be on His side! How about you?!

Keep memorizing Proverbs 3:5-6. If you already know these verses go ahead and work on 3:1-6. These will need to be memorized before you start on lesson 8.

Lesson 6 Worksheet

**"There is a way which seems right to a man,
but its end is the way of death." Proverbs 14:12**

The way that seems right to man is man's wisdom; this is different than God's wisdom. Let's see how they differ.

Read 1 Corinthians 1:18-31. This whole passage tells us that man's wisdom is not enough, but there is power in God's wisdom for the one who believes.

Decide whether the person in each of the following sentences is using God's wisdom or man's wisdom and circle your answer.

1. A man seeks the meanings of the stars to find out the future.
God's wisdom / Man's wisdom

2. A woman takes food to her neighbor and helps with the fight against cancer believing that her good works will get her into heaven.
God's wisdom / Man's wisdom

3. A woman takes food to her neighbor and helps with the fight against cancer because she believes that God has called her to reach out to others in love.
God's wisdom / Man's wisdom

4. Scientists are doing research to understand the nature of a black hole.
God's wisdom / Man's wisdom

5. A student studies hard and earns a doctorate in theology from Harvard hoping to please his parents and to get a good job.
God's wisdom / Man's wisdom

6. A child obeys her parents in deed, but grumbles about them in her heart.
God's wisdom / Man's wisdom

7. A drug user prays for forgiveness.
God's wisdom / Man's wisdom

8. A man insists on teaching about Jesus and is sent to prison.
God's wisdom / Man's wisdom

We must see life through God's eyes to understand His wisdom. That comes from first becoming a child of God and then reading His Word and spending time in prayer with Him.

More on Wisdom

Lesson 7

For the Lord gives wisdom;
From His mouth come knowledge and understanding.
Proverbs 2:6

We are going on a treasure hunt!! We will unearth the treasure of Proverbs chapter 2. But be careful! There are traps along the way!!

First we will need to fill up our backpacks with supplies.

Read Proverbs 2:1.

We need to put God's Word and His commandments into our pack. We must carry these along with us, stocking up when we run low. They are our food and will keep us going and give us energy on our quest.

What treasure are we seeking?

Our treasure has many names.

Read Proverbs 2:2-6 and fill in the blanks below to find out what we are searching for.

Make your ear attentive to ______________________.
Incline your heart to __________________________.
For if you cry for ___________________________,
Lift your voice for ___________________________;
If you seek her as silver
And search for her as for hidden treasures;
Then you will discern the ___________________ of the Lord
And discover the ________________________ of God.
For the Lord gives _____________________.

Wisdom goes by many names - but finding it always begins with the fear of the Lord and is gotten through perseverance and hard work. I never said hunting for treasure was easy!!

Notice that wisdom is personified here. That means that it is given characteristics of a person. Wisdom is called "her" and "she."

So, how valuable is this wisdom? In verse 4 we are told to look for her as if for silver and hidden treasures.

Read Proverbs 3:13-15. What is she, wisdom, compared to here?
1.
2.
3.

Gold is considered the most precious substance here on earth. Hundreds of years ago, salt used to be the most sought after commodity, and now we are in an age where oil is fought over. But more precious than any of these is God's wisdom. Remember that in heaven gold is nothing but paving stones for the roads! God's wisdom will last forever!

What training must you have to hunt for wisdom?

Look in Proverbs 2:7-8.

"He (God) stores up sound wisdom for the ___________________;
He is a shield to those who __________________ in ______________________,
Guarding the paths of justice,
And He preserves the way of _____________________ godly ones."

So, we must first be upright, walk in integrity, and belong to God. If you have asked Jesus into your heart to forgive your sins and to guide your life, then you, too, can look for wisdom!

If we were searching for gold, we would use the gold to buy our dreams! Maybe a boat or an airplane or new clothes!! But what good is getting wisdom? How will it benefit us?

Proverbs 2:7-12 gives us the answer. What good is wisdom? In verses 7-9 we see wisdom as a shield. It guards the paths of justice and preserves the way of God's children. Think about a shield for a minute.

What purpose does a shield have? ____________________________________

____

A shield protects, it can be used to push through enemy lines, it can be used for offense to strike the enemy. Wisdom is our spiritual shield. With it we can discern righteousness and justice and equity and every good course (vs. 9). That means that we can tell right from wrong, be fair and just, and know God's way for us that will lead to life.

Let's keep looking. **Check out verses 10-11.** Here we see more protection.

What will guard you? ____________________________

What will watch over you? ________________________

Don't you feel safe?

Read verse 12. What will you be safe from? ______________________________

These are the traps that we must watch out for. The first one is the people that we hang out with. It is important that your friends desire righteousness. (1 Corinthians 15:33 says that, ***"Bad company corrupts good morals".***) Stay away from the evil man or boy or girl!

The next trap is sin. Verses 12-19 describe our enemy. He is the one who speaks perverse things, leaves the path of righteousness, walks in the ways of darkness, delights in doing evil and is devious. Our enemy is shown here as an adulteress. Throughout the Bible, sin is personified as an adulteress – an unfaithful woman, someone who has a romantic relationship with someone besides her husband or has left her husband for another man. Sin is being unfaithful to our God (See verse 17).

Proverbs 2 ends with a promise!! If we seek wisdom, we will find her! And our reward will be that we will live in the land (eternity – heaven). And what's even better is that Jesus and the Father will be there and in Their presence is great joy!!

What do you think? Will go on a treasure hunt? Will you spend your life, your resources, your time, seeking for God's wisdom? I hope so, for all other treasure will rot and rust.

But store up for yourselves treasures in heaven,
where neither moth not rust destroys,
and where thieves do not break in or steal;
for where your treasure is, there your heart will be also.
Matthew 6:20-21

Keep memorizing your verses from Proverbs chapter 3.

**"...so that your faith would not rest on the wisdom of men,
but on the power of God."
1 Corinthians 2:5**

Read 1 Corinthians 2:1-16

In verse 1-5, Paul is talking about man's wisdom.

In verse 7 we see that God's wisdom has been a mystery.

In verse 10 we see that God has chosen to reveal to us the mystery of the wisdom of God.

What is this mystery? The answer is in Colossians 2:2-3. Write the mystery below.

____

Jesus Christ, Himself, is the mystery of God that was hidden from the rulers of earlier ages. The fact that God, Himself, in the form of Jesus Christ came to the earth as a man, lived a sinless life, and died on the cross as our substitute for death, that he rose again and ascended to the Father and is now sitting at the right hand of God so that we can be right with God through His blood is God's wisdom! His mystery continues as the Holy Spirit gives wisdom to people.

This mystery is wrapped up in 1 Corinthians 2:16. ***"But we have the mind of Christ."*** Wow!

Let's look closer at man's wisdom and God's wisdom as it is worked out in a Christian's life.

God wants us to have a relationship with Him, for us to listen to Him, and for us to obey Him. So often we decide what we want to do for God, rather than listening for what God wants us to do.

Let's pretend that we are going to fry an egg and try to not break the yolk. There is a difference if a task was your idea or God's idea. **Fill out the chart below.**

Objective	Whose assignment	Yolk broke (success or failure)	Yolk is whole (success or failure)
Don't break yolk	mine	________	________
Don't break yolk	God's	________	________

Your answers should have been failure and success for the first line and success and success for the second line. In our wisdom we failed if the yolk broke and were successful if it remained unbroken. But in God's wisdom, because He asked us to do it, we are a success no matter what the outcome is! God wants our obedience and the results are His to direct. There is freedom in this! **If we listen to God and obey we will always be successful in His eyes!** In this is wisdom.

Law and Grace

Lesson 8

Therefore there is now no condemnation for those who are in Christ Jesus.
Romans 8:1

If you were to commit a crime, what body of work would the lawyers and judges research to find out if you were guilty or not? ______________________________

That's right! They would go to the law of the land. Here in America that includes the Constitution and other laws. In the time of David and Solomon the law was the Ten Commandments and the other laws that God had given to Moses. The nation of Israel was judged according to how they kept these laws. You are under the law of the land of America, but you are also under the laws that your parents decided on for their home.

Have you ever broken a law? ____________________________

Why are there laws? Did God not want His people to have any fun? Did He want to rule them so that they had no choices? Does God want to be like a puppeteer, directing every action we take? Sometimes we feel that the law does just that. But, our God and our parents had a very different reason for setting down the law.

There are five reasons for law.

1. Protection
2. Provision
3. That we might know the lawgiver
4. That we might see our inability to keep the law
5. That we might see our need for a Savior

Name one law that you know of that is for your protection.

____

You might have put not going into the street to play, or that no one can come into your home without your consent or a search warrant, or even a set bedtime so that you are protected from not getting enough sleep and getting sick.

Name a law that is for your provision.

____

Laws for your provision might include that any child whose family's income is not above a certain level can get free food at school; driving laws are for our protection and provision by giving us an opportunity to get places without danger. The law that says that if we eat all of our dinner, we can have dessert is also for our provision.

If your family had a law that required you to never go outside, what would that tell you about the person making that law? ______________________________

If a law said that anyone who steals pencils should be shot, what would that tell you about the lawgiver? ____

The Lawgiver, God of the Bible, gave us laws that tell us about Him. He told the Israelites not to eat pork. He knew that pork contains parasites that the Israelites could not get rid of because they had no way of getting a fire hot enough. This tells us that God cared for them and did not want them to get sick.

God gave us the Ten Commandments because these laws kept the people in a right relationship with God and other men. This tells us that God wanted a relationship with them and that He cared how they treated each other. This shows us a loving and caring God.

In fact, all of the laws in the Old Testament tell us something about God.

These laws also show us our inability to keep the law. The Ten Commandments include obeying your Mom and Dad. Have you ever disobeyed? They include not giving false witness. Have you ever lied? The law shows us that we can't be perfect. But that's okay - remember that God sent us an answer to our problem. **Jesus!**

The law showed us that we needed another way to God because we could not be perfect or righteous on our own. God sent His perfect, righteous Son to die for our sins – to pay the penalty for our sins.

Now, we are no longer under the law, but under grace!! Yeah!! But what does that mean?

God's laws are there because He made us and knows what is best for us, but we are no longer judged by whether we follow those laws or not. **We should want to follow God's laws because we want to please God, we want what is best for ourselves, and we are thankful for God's gift of Jesus and eternal life.** Grace means that we won't be able to keep the law perfectly and that's okay, God loves us anyway! **God's love is based on the fact that He made us His children; it is not based on our performance!**

How does this last statement make you feel? (Circle one)

I don't believe it. Yeah!! Relieved Really?! But I am pretty good at doing things right!

Great, I am not perfect Then I can do what I want! I like being His child.

No matter how you feel or what you think - the truth is that God loves you just because you are His. God said so! **You are a prince or princess, a son or daughter of the King of Kings.** You may not always act like it, but that doesn't change the fact. Take a minute and tell God thanks for His unconditional Father Love.

This does not give us the right to act any way that we want to, however. As a child of the king, we must learn to act like royalty. We can find out how we should act by reading the New Testament letters written by Paul and looking at how Jesus acted on earth and how God acts.

Tell your memory verses, Proverbs 3:5-6 or 3:1-6 to a parent or an adult. Good Job!!

Here is our next verse to memorize. It is short so it shouldn't take you too long. But it is very important!

Therefore there is now no condemnation
for those who are in Christ Jesus.
Romans 8:1

See if you can memorize this one by lesson 10.

Lesson 8 Worksheet

**For by grace you have been saved through faith;
and that not of yourselves, it is the gift of God…
Ephesians 2:8**

If you could write the laws for your own life, what would they be? Write them below, but think about whether each law is for your provision or for your protection and what they teach someone about the lawgiver (you). An example of a law of provision would be, "We must have family night each Friday and everyone in the family must come." This also tells someone that family is important to the lawgiver.

1.
2.
3.
4.
5.
6.

Now, what should be the punishment for breaking each law?

1.
2.
3.
4.
5.
6.

Decide whether you would extend grace or stick to the law. For example, in my first illustration, if my sister didn't make it to family night because she was scheduled to work, would you make her miss a meal and have to take out the garbage for a week, or would you forgive her, understand, and love her just like she is?

I would extend _____________________. (Grace or Law)

That's law and grace. God knew that we can't be perfect and holy like He is, but He still wants to have a relationship with us and so He decided to extend grace to each of us that have believed in His Son, Jesus.

Paul talks a lot about this in the book of Romans. It is a little hard to understand, but you should try to read through it and begin to make sense of it. The book of Romans will make you really grateful for God's grace. And remember, God extended grace to you, so you should be willing to extend God's grace to others!

God's grace – When God gave us what we didn't deserve (forgiveness and righteousness).
God's mercy – When God didn't give us what we deserved (death and judgment).

Who God Says You Are

Lesson 9

I am fearfully and wonderfully made...
How precious are Your thoughts to me, O God,
How vast is the sum of them!
If I should count them, they would outnumber the sand.
Psalm 139:14a, 17-18a

Does God lie? NO!! And He says that you are precious!! He says that you are wonderfully made!! He calls you His child!! Wow!

Let's see what else God says about you. **Look up these verses and fill in the blanks.**

Matthew 5:13 ***"You are the ______________ of the earth..."*** (You make life more tastier in contrast to the dull taste of life without God!)

Matthew 5:14 ***"You are the __________________ of the world."*** (You make others see clearly in contrast to the darkness of the mind without God!)

John 8:32 ***"And you will know the truth and the truth will make you ________________."*** (Free from sin, shame, guilt, and life apart from God!)

Romans 1:7 ***"...to all who are __________________ of God..."***

Romans 8:16-17 ***"The Spirit Himself testifies with our spirit that we are _______________ of God, and if children, _______________ also, heirs of God and fellow heirs with Christ..."*** (An heir is someone who will receive all the material goods when someone dies. In this case we will receive all of God's goodness and blessings when we die!"

Romans 8:37 ***"But in all these things we overwhelmingly ____________________ through Him who loved us."*** (His love makes us conquerors!!)

2 Corinthians 5:17 ***"Therefore if anyone is in Christ, he is a new __________________..."*** (That means that we are no longer held accountable for what we did before we knew Christ and now we have the ability to make better choices!!)

2 Corinthians 5:20 ***"Therefore, we are ________________________________ for Christ..."*** (An ambassador is someone who represents their country to another country. God trusts us to go and tell others by our words and actions about His love and salvation.)

This one is way cool!! Check out 2 Corinthians 5:21 ***"He made Him who knew no sin to be sin on our behalf, so that we might become the ______________________________ of God in Him."*** (You are righteous because Jesus declared you to be with His death.)

Zechariah 2:*8* ***"…for he who touches you, touches the ______________ of His eye."*** (God is talking to the Jews here, but as Christians we were grafted into, or made a part of the nation of Israel, God's chosen people.)

Now, go back through these verses and write a list of who God says you are.
I am…

1. Wonderfully made
2.
3.
4.
5.
6.
7.
8.
9.
10.
11.
12.

There are a lot more words to describe what God thinks about you. Look for them as you read through the Scriptures. Psalms and the New Testament are full of them!!

Lastly, let's look at Psalm 37:23-24. **Read these verses.**

God delights in you!! When you fall, not if, but when (God knows you are human and that you will mess up. He just asks you to come quickly to Him and say you are sorry), He will be there to pick you up, hold your hand and see you on your way again. God is a loving Father who is close by to protect you and help you just like a parent that holds their toddler's hand while he is learning to walk. He knows Mom or Dad will pick him up and love him and set him up straight when he stumbles or falls.

So that's who you are according to God. Will you agree with Him or continue to listen to Satan's lies? It's your choice and it will make a difference in how you see yourself and how you act. **Be the prince or princess that you are!!**

Review your definition of wisdom and Proverbs 3:5-6. Romans 8:1 is due before your next lesson!

Because you are sons [and daughters],
God has sent forth the Spirit of His Son into our hearts, crying,
"Abba! Father!"
Galatians 4:6

When you were born again you became a prince or a princess!! God is the King of all Kings and you are His son or daughter! You may not always feel like royalty. You may not always act like royalty. But that doesn't change the fact that you are, indeed, an heir to the throne. **Read Ephesians 2:1-6. According to verse 6 where are you seated right now?**

____

No, not in your chair or on the floor! You are seated with Christ in the heavenly places. That is your position as God's child.

Draw a picture of you sitting with Jesus in heaven.

When you mess up or don't feel like God or anyone else loves you, turn back to this picture. This is where you belong. Make things right with God and picture yourself once again as His beloved Prince or Princess.

Self-esteem

Lesson 10

But as many as received Him,
to them He gave the right to become children of God,
even to those who believe in His name.
John 1:12

Fill in the blanks: I am ________________________ (adjective)

I am loved because ____________________________________

I am important because _________________________________

Others think I am ______________________________________

So many of us think that our worth is based upon what others think about us, what we think about ourselves, or our performance (whether we can play basketball, or dance, or be good, or always smile, etc.) **This is a lie from Satan!!**

Let's talk about Satan for a minute. He was the most beautiful and powerful angel created by God. But he got it into his head that he wanted to be worshipped like God. God said, "No!" and threw Satan, then called Lucifer, out of heaven. One-third of the angels went with him. We call these former angels, demons. Satan hates God and wants to keep us from worshipping God. He will do anything to keep us from having a right relationship with God!

Read 1 Peter 5:8 ***"…your adversary the devil, prowls around like a roaring lion, seeking someone to devour."***

He does this through false religion, idolatry (making anything more important than God), and lies. He is the great deceiver. He twists the truth. Satan would have you believe that God can't love you unless you are perfect, that you are no good if others don't like you.

Satan is also tricky. He talks to us, but makes us think that his words are our own. For example a thought might come into your head: "I am no good." "I am so stupid!" "I can't do anything right!" "No wonder no one likes me, I hate me!!" "I really messed up." "I don't deserve to be loved." All of these statements are in first person. That means that they sound like you are saying them, when really Satan plants these thoughts in your mind. You probably wouldn't listen to them if Satan said, "You are…"

What lie does Satan put into your mind that you tend to believe? ____________

____

2 Corinthians has the solution to these lies. **Read 2 Corinthians 10:3-5.**

> ***"For though we walk in the flesh, we do not war according to the flesh, for the weapons of our warfare are not of the flesh, but divinely powerful for the destruction of fortresses. We are destroying speculations and every lofty thing raised up against the knowledge of God, and we are taking every thought captive to the obedience of Christ."***

(Speculations are when we ask, "What if…?" Or, "If only…")

When Satan's lies come into our minds we are to identify them and destroy them. Lies are destroyed with truth. Just like light and darkness cannot be found together at the same time, neither can lies and truth. **Truth will make the lies flee!!**

We can fight against Satan's attacks!! We have weapons!! We have power!!

So here are the steps to remembering that you are first and above all else a forgiven, precious, loved child of God.

1. Recognize the lie
2. Replace the lie with God's truth

How do we recognize a lie? A lie is any thought that we have that does not agree with God. Lies tell us we are no good, we should give up, we are unlovable, etc.

To know God's truth, you need to be studying His Word, learning all you can about Him. Here are some verses that you can use against Satan's lies. (I took these from a book called Search For Significance by Dr. Robert McGee.)

Truth: I am deeply loved by God.

> 1 John 4:9-10 ***"By this the love of God was manifested in us, that God has sent His only begotten Son into the world so that we might live through Him. In this is love, not that we loved God, but that He love us and sent His Son to be the propitiation (atoning sacrifice) for our sins."***

Truth: I am completely forgiven and am fully pleasing to God.

> Romans 5:1 ***"Therefore, having been justified by faith, we have peace with God through our Lord Jesus Christ."***

Practical Proverbs 

Truth: I am totally accepted by God.

Colossians 1:21-*22* ***"And although you were formerly alienated and hostile in mind, engaged in evil deeds, yet, He has now reconciled you in His fleshly body through death, in order to present you before Him holy and blameless and beyond reproach."***

Truth: I am a new creation, complete in Christ.

2 Corinthians 5:17 ***"Therefore if anyone is in Christ, he is a new creature: the old things passed away; behold, new things have come.***

Fill in the blanks for your memory verse: Romans 8:1

________________________ there is now _____ ___________________________ for those ___________ _____________ ________ Christ Jesus.

For by grace you have been saved through faith;
and that not of yourselves, it is the gift of God;
not as a result of works, so that no one may boast.
Ephesians 2:8-9

What do people compliment you for? Is it your looks, your sweet smile, your athletic ability, your singing, or something else? ____

Because people notice this about you, do you work extra hard at this attribute? _______

A girl in my class at college was sweet and naturally bubbly and cute. She won a contest that the students had and was voted the prettiest girl in the class. After that she changed, she started wearing a lot of make-up, being more concerned about her clothes, and she lost the happy-go-lucky perkiness that everyone thought was so attractive in the first place!
Dr. Robert McGee, the author of Search for Significance, says that most of us follow the **world's idea for our self-esteem.** He sums this up in this equation:

Your worth = Your performance + Others' opinions

Do you agree with this statement? _______________________

How important is your performance to you? Do you get mad when you do something wrong? (Circle one – 1 being not at all and 10 being very important)

1 2 3 4 5 6 7 8 9 10

How important is other people's opinion about you? (Circle one - 1 being not at all and 10 being very important)

1 2 3 4 5 6 7 8 9 10

Write true or false next to these statements: (Take a minute and really think how you respond in situations.)

_____ 1. Those who fail are unworthy of love and deserve to be blamed and condemned.

_____ 2. I must meet certain standards to feel good about myself.

_____ 3. If others fail it is okay because God loves them anyway.

_____ 4. I must be accepted by certain others to feel good about myself.

_____ 5. If I mess up, I can forgive myself because God has forgiven me.

_____ 6. I am what I am. I cannot change. I am hopeless.

God's Word would say that numbers 1, 2, 4, and 6 are false and numbers 3 and 5 are true.

Many Christians know this in their heads, but have not really experienced these truths in their hearts and lives. A Christian learns to experience these truths by reminding himself/herself over and over again about the truths of God's Word.

This is God's truth about you:

MY IDENTITY IN CHRIST
BECAUSE OF CHRIST'S REDEMPTION,
I AM A NEW CREATION OF INFINITE WORTH.

I AM DEEPLY LOVED,
I AM COMPLETELY FORGIVEN,
I AM FULLY PLEASING,
I AM TOTALLY ACCEPTED BY GOD,
I AM ABSOLUTELY COMPLETE IN CHRIST!

WHEN MY PERFORMANCE
REFLECTS MY NEW IDENTITY IN CHRIST,
THAT REFLECTION IS DYNAMICALLY UNIQUE!

THERE HAS NEVER BEEN ANOTHER PERSON LIKE ME
IN THE HISTORY OF MANKIND,
NOR WILL THERE EVER BE!
GOD HAS MADE ME AN ORIGINAL,
ONE OF A KIND, REALLY SOMEBODY!

Dr. Robert McGee

This is great to memorize. Remember, you are a prince or a princess, even when you don't act like one or feel like one! The King of Kings is your father!!

Psalm 1 and Proverbs 1

Lesson 11

Wisdom shouts in the street,
She lifts her voice in the square.
Proverbs 1:20

Turn to Psalm 1. This is a great Psalm to memorize. We will be working on that over the next few lessons. Let's start by looking at the first two verses.

> ***How blessed is the man that does not walk in the counsel of the wicked,***
> ***Nor stand in the path of sinners,***
> ***Nor sit in the seat of scoffers,***
>
> ***But his delight is in the law of the Lord,***
> ***And in His law he meditates day and night.***

Notice the progression of the action in the first verse: walk, stand, sit.

When we are walking we may notice something that we pass by, then we stand to gawk at it, and finally decide to move on or sit and partake in the event. Sin is the same way. First we walk along and it will catch our eye, "Hmm, that looks interesting." Then we stand and watch others participating in it or we stand and daydream of our participation in the activity. Lastly, we sit and indulge!!

Now let's turn to Proverbs 1:10-19 and see this same sin entice or encourage us. Read these verses.

Verse 10 reminds us that **we have a choice**: ***"My son (or daughter), if sinners entice you, do not ______________________________."***

Notice here that temptation leads to a choice. **Temptation is not sin**. We all face temptations every day, **how we respond to those temptations is what leads to sin or righteousness.**

Verse 13 promises great reward for sin. Moses knew that sin can be fun and that sin can bring pleasure and rewards. But he also knew that the fun **only lasts a moment** and when we choose sin, we are turning away from even greater reward and eternal pleasure.

Read Hebrews 11:24-26.

What rewards could Moses have had? ______________________________
What reward was Moses looking to? ______________________________

Practical Proverbs

That's right. He chose a relationship and obedience to Christ over the riches of Egypt. Remember, he was considered a son by Pharaoh himself. He could have had riches, and palaces, girls, and power. He chose instead hardship and the leadership over a group of people that weren't very obedient. He chose desert wandering over a life of ease and pleasure. Following God held greater promise for eternity and joy in the relationship with God while Moses was here on earth.

We look at those in this world that have chosen sin and sometimes it seems that they have it all – riches, houses, ease, power, fun, etc… But remember that the things of this earth are only temporary and that the things of God are for forever!

Read 2 Corinthians 4:17-18.

"For momentary light affliction is producing for us an eternal weight of glory far beyond all comparison, while we look not at the things which are _____________, but at the things which are _________ ___________; for the things which are seen are temporal, but the things which are not seen are eternal."

So, we have a choice.

According to Proverbs 1:19 and 1:32, what is the result of a life of evil?

____

According to Proverbs 1:33, what is the result of listening to Wisdom and making Godly choices? ____

Read all of Proverbs 1:20-33.

Wisdom calls out to whom? ____

Wisdom calls out to the naive, scoffers, and fools. In other words, we don't have to be good enough before we turn to God and listen to His wisdom. We call out to God when we are naïve, needy, sinful, ashamed, and hurting. He promises to hear us and answer our cry. But if He calls us and we refuse Him, then He will not rescue us from our messes. We will instead reap what we have sown! (Reaping is taking in the harvest and sowing is putting the seeds into the ground. If you sow a corn seed, you will reap corn. If you sow repentance, you will reap forgiveness.)

Recite Romans 8:1 to a parent.

Start memorizing Psalm 1:1-2. It might help to act it out or draw pictures next to key words.

**Blessed be the God and Father of our Lord Jesus Christ,
who has blessed us with every spiritual blessing
in the heavenly places in Christ.
Ephesians 1:3**

A great Chinese teacher named Watchman Nee wrote a short book called Sit, Walk, Stand. This book was based on the book of Ephesians. As you go through the book of Ephesians you realize that we are seated next to Jesus in heaven, that you are to walk in His ways, and that you are to stand against the devil. The first 3 chapters of Ephesians talk about sitting with Jesus.

Look at Ephesians 3:14-21. These verses tell us why it is so important to take the time to sit in the presence of God.

> **According to verse 16 what will God grant to us?**
> ***"…that He would grant you, according to the riches of His glory, to be _____________ with __________________ through His _____________ in the inner man…"***
>
> **This will allow Christ to dwell in our hearts through faith which will lead us to being what?** (vs.17) ***"… __________________ and _____________________ in love."***

Being rooted and grounded in love will make us able to understand the breadth and length and height and depth of God's love.

> That love, according to verse 19, "***surpasses*** ______________" and will fill us up with the fullness of God!!
>
> **Write out verse 20:** ____
> ____
> ____
> ____

Do you sometimes think that you ask too much of God? I think that He wants to bless us with so much more love and peace and joy than we can even begin to understand!

Once you have sat in God's presence, then you are ready to walk. Ephesians 4:1 says:

> ***"Therefore I… implore you to walk in a manner worthy of the calling with which you have been called."***

We cannot successfully walk the Christian life without being empowered by the Holy Spirit. Sitting with Jesus gives us the power to walk! Look at Ephesians 5:1-2:

> ***"Therefore be imitators of God, as beloved children; and walk in love…"***

Practical Proverbs

We walk successfully each day by being imitators of Christ. We can love others, comfort others, forgive others, be pure, be wise, and know truth as we walk because we have first sat with Christ. Once we have sat with Christ, walked in love like Christ, then we are ready to take a stand!

Read Ephesians 6:10-18.

Here is where we stand against the devil and his angels. So many Christians fail because they try to stand, but have never walked. They try to walk, but have never sat. Don't let that be your story. Take the time now to sit and learn from the Word of God each day and go out ready to walk in His ways. When you need to stand, God will empower you with His Sword (the word of God) to take the victory!!

Label the parts of armor below from Ephesians 6:10-18. But remember, a knight is first a student before he earns his knighthood!

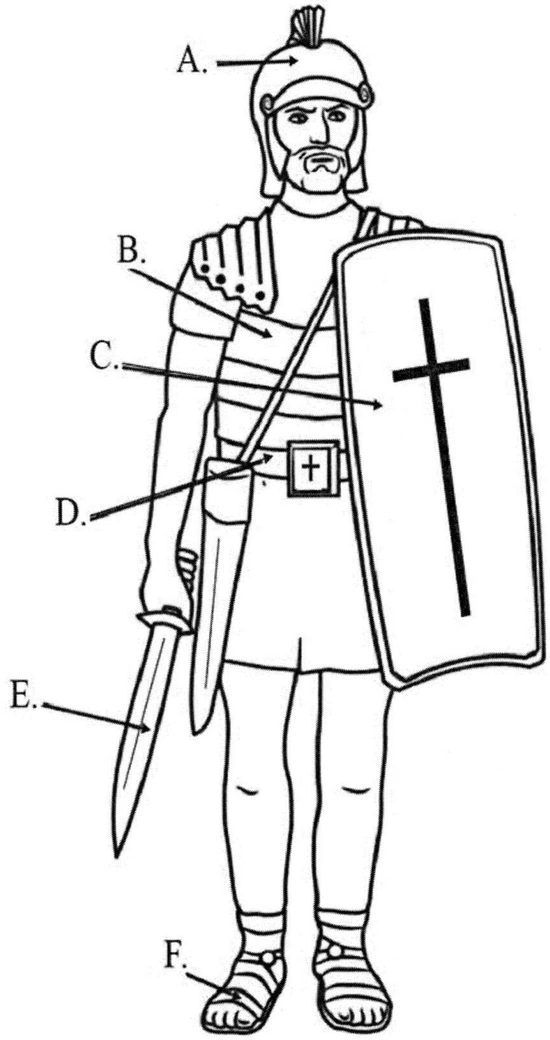

A.
B.
C.
D.
E.
F.

A.____________________________

B.____________________________

C.____________________________

D.____________________________

E.____________________________

F.____________________________

Psalm 1 continued

Lesson 12

But his delight is in the law of the Lord,
And in His law he meditates day and night.
He will be like a tree firmly planted by streams of water,
Which yields its fruit in its season
And its leaf does not wither;
And in whatever he does, he prospers.
Psalm 1:2-3

Yesterday we looked at the first part of Psalm 1. Today we will look at the rest of it. You will have a few more days to work on memorizing this Psalm.

Draw below a picture of a tree planted by a stream of water with fruit on it.

Let's talk about your tree. It should be firmly planted into good soil. A tree gets nutrition from the soil as well as a firm hold so that it won't fall over. The Word of God is to be our soil. To keep holding firm, we must keep reading the Word.

Your tree is planted by a stream of water. Water in the New Testament symbolizes the Holy Spirit. Now, if you are born again, having asked Jesus to come into your heart and be in control, then you have the Holy Spirit living inside of you. But! You have to invite the Holy Spirit to work in your life. You have to go to the stream of water and drink from it just like your tree is doing. You have to receive the rain. Just being happy knowing that the Holy Spirit is there, but never talking to Him or listening to Him, would be like a man dying of thirst as he stands next to your stream of water!!

The next thing that your tree needs is sunshine. Draw a sun in your picture if you haven't already. The sun is needed for photosynthesis or the making of food for energy. You need to receive the Son as well to grow and be healthy! Just accepting Jesus is not enough, you have to keep on lifting your arms up to Him in prayer and praise to receive the benefits of being His.

Practical Proverbs 

Okay, let's talk about the fruit. Turn to Galatians 5:22 and list the fruit of the Spirit below.

1.
2.
3.
4.
5.
6.
7.
8.
9.

Now, have you ever thought, "I need to try to be more loving? More patient? More kind? Etc...?" Probably, we all have. But let's think about this for a minute. Have you ever seen a tree *trying* to bear fruit? Have you seen a peach tree grunt and groan *trying* to pop out fruit?

No, the tree puts its roots down deep into the soil and water and spreads its branches to the sun and the fruit grows naturally!! That is how we are to grow fruit as well. As we put our roots deep into the Word of God and into the Spirit and we spend time reaching for Jesus, the Son, fruit will begin to develop naturally. One day you will look back in astonishment and you will have become more loving, more patient, more kind, etc...!

This brings joy!! Being in God's presence is the way to find love, joy, and peace!! Are you staying firmly planted? What is your plan to read your Bible every day? Are you reading a particular book? Studying a person? Working through a Bible study? There are lots of ways to read the Word of God – just make sure that you are doing it!!

Take just a minute and look at Psalm 1:4. Chaff is a coating that covers a wheat berry or seed. At the time that this Psalm was written, the farmer would literally throw the wheat up into the air by the handfuls and the wind would blow off the chaff and the wheat would fall to the ground. Chaff is easily blown away, is dry, and has no value. **Read Proverbs 10:25.** Don't be chaff!!

Work on memorizing Psalm 1:1-2 today. We will add verse 3 next lesson.

In the beginning was the Word,
and the Word was with God,
and the Word was God.
John 1:1

The battle for life and death is played out in the mind. Your thoughts, your will, your actions all work to make you who you are and who you will become. Psalm 1 says that we are to meditate in the law day and night. Psalms was written while the Israelites were under the Old Mosaic Covenant. The Israelites were expected to know the law and keep the law. When they messed up there was a whole code of sacrifices that had to be made so that the blood of an animal would take away their guilt. When Jesus came, He gave us a new covenant – one that is about relationship not about keeping the law. **His blood now covers our guilt for all time!**

But as New Covenant believers, we do still need to meditate on the law and the New Covenant (as given in the New Testament of your Bible). The law shows us the heart of God, and the New Testament teaches us how to live out a relationship with our amazing God. Hebrews 4:12 says,

> ***"The Word of God is __________________ and ______________________ and sharper than any two-edged sword, and piercing as far as the division of soul and spirit, of both joints and marrow, and able to judge the thoughts and intentions of the heart."***

There is power in the Word of God!! What does the Word have the power to do?

1. **The word of God transforms us when we use it to renew our minds.** The Word of God leads us to understand and be able to live out the will of God.

   Romans 12:2 ***"And do not be conformed to this world, but be __________________ by the renewing of your mind, so that you may prove what the will of God is, that which is good and acceptable and perfect."***

2. **The Word of God teaches, gives reproof and correction, and trains us in righteousness.**

   2 Timothy 3:16 ***"All Scripture is inspired by God and profitable for ___________________, for ________________, for ________________________, for _______________________ in righteousness…"***

3. **The Word of God makes its student adequate and equipped for every good work.**

2 Timothy 3:17 ***"…so that the man of God may be adequate, equipped for every good work."***

4. **The Word of God is powerful against Satan and his demons.**

Ephesians 6:17 ***"And take…the sword of the Spirit, which is the word of God."***

How important do you think it is that you read, study, meditate on, and memorize the word of God? ____

If you have never had a regular time in the Bible, now is a good time to start. I usually have one bookmark in the Psalms, one in the gospels (Matthew, Mark, Luke, and John) or Acts, and one in the New Testament letters. I don't read all of these every day, but that gives me a firm foundation. I prefer to read the Old Testament like a book, absorbing its stories. I also choose a passage of Scripture to memorize and work on as well.

What is your plan? Write it out below.

When will you meet with God?

Where will you meet with God?

What book of the Bible or devotional are you going to use?

Make sure you pray as you learned in lesson 5.

Some people write down their prayers and then write down the answers when they come!! A journal is good if you like to write. I find I pray better when I am writing out my prayers. You might choose to write down what you learn or what you hear God say to you!

Wisdom and Foolishness

Lesson 13

A wise son makes a father glad,
But a foolish son is a grief to his mother.
Proverbs 10:1

Today we are going to look at some comparisons. Proverbs compares the ***characteristics*** of wisdom and foolishness and the ***results*** of wisdom and foolishness. Let's make a chart. You will look up the verses and fill in the chart according to the verse. All the verses are found in Proverbs. I did a couple to get you started. (The biblical "son" also includes girls!)

	Wisdom (Righteous)		**Foolishness (Wicked)**	
	Characteristics	Results	Characteristics	Results
10:3		will not go hungry		cravings will not be satisfied
10:5	Gathers in summer		Sleeps in harvest	
10:6		blessings	mouth conceals violence	
10:7				
10:9				
10:10				
10:11				
10:14				
10:16				
10:21				
10:24				
10:30				

Take a minute and read down your chart, one subtopic at a time. For example, read Wisdom: Characteristics, then read Foolishness: Characteristics. Now read Wisdom: Results and Foolishness: Results. Which do you choose? That's right. Wisdom or foolishness is a choice to the believer. A non-believer has no choice – they will act foolishly.

Draw a caterpillar.

Can he fly? No, all he can do is walk on the ground. Now draw a butterfly.

Did you make your butterfly fly? If not your picture is not wrong - a butterfly can choose to walk on the ground, but how sad!! If I could fly, I wouldn't want to be down in the dirt!

A non-believer will make foolish choices; he doesn't know wisdom. He is stuck in sin like our caterpillar is stuck on the ground. But, as a believer, you have a choice!! Are you going to continue walking in sin, or, like our butterfly, are you going to soar above life's troubles and temptations and choose wisdom? What's it going to be: wisdom or foolishness?

Keep memorizing Psalm 1:1-2, but let's add verse 3. You can draw pictures next to this section.

> **"He will be like a tree firmly planted by streams of water,**
>
> **Which yields its fruit in its season**
>
> **And its leaf does not wither;**
>
> **And in whatever he does, he prospers."**

Lesson 13 Worksheet

The memory of the righteous is blessed,
But the name of the wicked will rot.
Proverbs 10:7

For today's worksheet, you will need two highlighters of differing colors. I want you to decide which color will stand for foolishness and which color will stand for wisdom. Then read Proverbs 11 and highlight the lines, one by one, according to wisdom and foolishness. If you don't want to mark up your Bible, then copy chapter 11 and highlight the copy. You can also go back and highlight chapter 10 if you want to.

For example:

11:1 A false balance is an abomination to the Lord, (should be in your foolish color).
But a just weight is His delight. (should be in your wisdom color).

After you have highlighted the wisdom and foolishness lines, go back and try to determine why some are wise and some are foolish. For example, in the verse above, why is a false balance and abomination and a just weight God's delight? ______________________________

____

____

Remember that wisdom is Jesus. He always makes the heart of God glad. God's character demands truth, and righteousness, and purity.

Receiving Instruction

Lesson 14

A wise man will hear and increase in learning,
And a man of understanding will acquire wise counsel…
The fear of the Lord is the beginning of knowledge;
Fools despise wisdom and instruction.
Proverbs 1:5-7

Think back to the last time you were disciplined for doing something that you shouldn't have done. What was your attitude after receiving punishment?

Were you grateful or resentful? ______________________________________

Read and fill in the following verses from Proverbs.

Proverbs 9:7-12

"He who corrects a scoffer gets dishonor for himself,
And he who reproves a __________________ *man gets insults for himself.*

Do not reprove a __________________,
Or he will _______________ *you,*
Reprove a wise man and he will _____________ *you.*

Give instruction to a wise man and he will be still wiser,
Teach a __________________ *man and he will* ________________ *his learning.*

The fear of the Lord is the beginning of wisdom,
And the knowledge of the Holy One is understanding.

For by Mee your days will be multiplied, and years of life will be added to you.

*If you are*_______________, *you are wise for yourself,*
And if you _________________, *you alone will bear it".*

A scoffer is someone who laughs and makes fun of another. If you call your parent a name or blame your punishment on them, then you are a scoffer.

There are two ways people respond when they are instructed or rebuked.

1. They listen and prayerfully discern whether or not they need to change.
2. They don't listen and keep doing what they are doing and will develop a hard or rebellious heart.

How you respond probably depends some on whether or not you respect the person giving you advice. We will talk about respect later on, but **respecting your Mom and Dad is not a suggestion, it is a command.**

Let's look at what else Proverbs says about listening and receiving instruction. Fill in the following verses.

Proverbs 1:8 ***"Hear, my son, your ______________________ instruction***
And do not forsake your ______________________ teaching…"

Proverbs 2:1-5 ***"My son, if you will ______________________ my words***
And treasure my commandments within you,
Make your ear ______________________ to wisdom,
______________________ your heart to understanding;
For if you cry for discernment,
Lift your voice for understanding;
If you seek her as silver,
And search for her as for hidden treasures;
____________ you will discern the fear of the LORD And discover the knowledge of God."

Proverbs 3:1-2 ***"My son, do not forget my ______________________,***
But let your heart keep my ______________________;
For length of days and years of life
And peace they will add to you."

Proverbs 4:1-2 ***"Hear, O sons, the instruction of a father,***
And __________ ______________ that you may gain understanding,
For I give you sound teaching;
Do not abandon my instruction."

Proverbs 5:1 ***"My son, ____________ __________________ to my wisdom,***
__________________ your ear(lean towards) to my understanding;
That you may observe discretion
And your lips may reserve knowledge."

Notice how the second, third, fourth, fifth, and seventh chapters of Proverbs start with the same thought. Out of love for the son, the father is saying, "Hey, listen up! This is important and you need to hear this!" In the English language we have words that are either comparative or superlative.

For example: You may be tall, but she is taller, and he is tallest of all.

The –er and –est ending makes the word carry more importance. The Hebrew and Greek languages did not have this ability by adding endings, so instead, they repeated words for emphasis and importance. The most recognizable is found in Isaiah 6:3 – ***"Holy, holy, holy, is the Lord of hosts."*** God is the holiest of all!!

So, how important do you think it was for the author of Proverbs, Solomon, to get the attention of his son and to say "Hey, listen up!"? "My son" is found 11 times in the first 7 chapters of Proverbs. That's really super superlative!!

Solomon definitely wanted his son to listen to and act upon his discipline and advice. But there was Someone else that he told his son to listen to as well.

Proverbs 3:11-12 ***"My son, do not _______________ the discipline of the***
_______________ or loathe His reproof,
For whom the LORD loves He reproves,
Even as a father corrects the son in whom he delights."

Yep, God will discipline us, too.

Read Hebrews 12:6. What is the motive behind God's discipline? _______________

What do you think is the motive behind your parents' discipline? ____________

That's right, it's love!! They love you enough to want you to do things that will enable you to grow and be strong and they discipline you when you do things that are harmful or immature.

Take a minute and thank God and your parents for disciplining you. Next time they have to punish you, remember to honor them and not be resentful.

Keep working on memorizing Psalm 1:1-3! You have two more lessons to get it!

Poverty and shame will come to him who neglects discipline,
But he who regards reproof will be honored.
Proverbs 13:18

It takes humility to accept discipline. Check out these verses in Proverbs on humility and match the first half of each verse to the second half and then the verse to its chapter and verse.

Address	First Half	Second Half
Prov. 11:2	"Proud," "Haughty," "Scoffer," are his names,	But with the humble is wisdom.
Prov. 12:9	But when pride comes, then comes dishonor	Than he who honors himself and lacks bread.
Prov. 16:5	Everyone who is proud in heart is an abomination to the Lord;	And a haughty spirit before stumbling.
Prov. 16:18	Before destruction the heart of man is haughty	Are riches, honor and life.
Prov. 16:19	It is better to be humble in spirit with the lowly	But humility goes before honor.
Prov. 18:12	Pride goes before destruction,	Assuredly, he will not be unpunished.
Prov. 21:2	Better is he who is lightly esteemed and has a servant	Than to divide the spoil with the proud.
Prov. 21:24	The reward of humility and the fear of the Lord	Who acts with insolent pride.
Prov. 22:4	Every man's way is right in his own eyes,	But the Lord weighs the heart.

Trust

Lesson 15

Trust in the Lord with all your heart
And do not lean on your own understanding.
In all your ways acknowledge Him,
And He will make your paths straight.
Proverbs 3:5-6

Pretend that your house is on fire!! Oh no!!

What will you save? ____

Did you pick money, food, a favorite outfit, a toy or a picture? Could you live without the thing that you chose?

If your answer is, "No," then you have put your trust in something besides God. That is idolatry.

My son is a soccer player. My niece is a ballerina. If Ethan could no longer play soccer or Callie could no longer dance, would they be okay? I asked them that question and they were both able to answer, "Yes! God is in control and He will have something better planned for me!!" **That's trust**. What about you? If there were no food in the pantry or refrigerator, there were no clothes in your closet, all your closest friends and family died, and you were injured, would you still be okay?

Let's look at Job for a minute. This man walked righteously before God. Job lived before Jesus came to the earth, but there were many people in the Old Testament that walked by faith in God's promise to send the Messiah. They lived with integrity and in a relationship with God and by their faith were considered righteous.

Satan decided that Job is only righteous and walking with God because only good things happen to him. He asked God for permission to test Job. Notice here that God did not test Job; Satan did. God gave Satan authority over the earth for a time until Jesus returns. So Satan did his dirty work with Job. His ten children were killed, his servants were slaughtered, and his livestock was stolen. Job responds to these tragedies by worshipping God. Job 1:22 says that, ***"Through all this Job did not sin nor did he blame God."***

But that wasn't enough for Satan, he went back to God and asked permission to make Job really sick. God said, "Okay," as long as Satan does not kill Job. Job got boils all over his skin. Boils are pus pockets that burn and hurt. Job's wife told him to curse God and die. Job responded, ***"Shall we indeed accept good from God and not accept adversity?"*** In all this, Job did not sin with his lips (Job 2:10).

Job had three friends that accused him of having bad attitudes and wrong doings, but Job knew that he was innocent.

Eventually, Job called on God to give account of all these bad things that had happened to him. God answers that He, God made this world, He set the stars in place, He controls the waters and the gates of death. In other words, "Job, who are you to question Me?" Job realizes how silly it is to think that he could understand God. **He decides to just trust God.**

Read Job 42:1-6. Job repents of pride and **allows God to be the one in control, on the throne, and in charge of his life.** That's trust! God, in His goodness restores Job's fortunes times two!

Look up Isaiah 55:8-9. Fill in the blanks:

> ***"For My ____________________ are not your ______________________________,***
> ***Nor are your ______________ My __________________," declares the Lord.***
> ***For as the heavens are higher than the earth,***
> ***So are My _________________ higher than your ____________,***
> ***And My __________________ than your _____________________.***

Trust is believing that God is who He says He is and that He will do what He says He will do even when circumstances seem out of control; even when we don't *feel* that God is in control.

What do you need to trust God with today? ____________________________________

God has seen me through the divorce of my parents, 20+ moves, losing a baby, 4 back surgeries because of spina bifida, and much more. He has been through life with me and there has been great joy in the midst!! He promises to never leave us or forsake us. That's enough and no matter what, I am okay!!

Choose today to trust God. Read Philippians 4:6. Being anxious and worrying is not trusting!! Pray and wait upon God. He will be there!!

One more lesson before Psalm 1:1-3 is due!! Are you ready?

Incline your ear and hear the words of the wise,
And apply your mind to my knowledge;
For it will be pleasant if you keep them within you,
That they may be ready on your lips.
So that your trust may be in the Lord...
Proverbs 22:17-19a

Unscramble these words to find what things people put their trust in.

1. noyem ______________________________
2. elhhat ______________________________
3. lefs ______________________________
4. rhotes ______________________________
5. stelnat ______________________________
6. yubate ______________________________
7. nllgiecitene ______________________________
8. dregas ______________________________
9. snapl ______________________________
10. turfeu ______________________________

I was a fast pitch softball player that trained for the Pan Am games, then I tore up my shoulder.

I was first chair French horn player, then I had back surgeries and couldn't hold my horn.

I was tall and skinny, then I had 5 children and lost two inches in height from those back surgeries.

I was loved by my relatives, then they decided not to love me anymore.

My husband made good money, then he went back to school and couldn't find a job.

I was an A student, then didn't get to finish college.

But, God already knew my needs and provided for every one of them!!

Pain is only for the day.
My children are the joy of my life.
God's love and fatherhood is real and never fails!
My husband finished school and God has always provided!
I didn't go to college, but I am writing books and speaking all over the United States!

What is your story? What are you trusting in?

____

____

____

____

____

Give these things to God and know that you will be okay even if…

Because you have a God that is bigger than all of that!!

There are only three things that will last forever: God, people (in heaven or hell), and God's Word (truth).

Make sure that your trust is in that which will last and will never forsake you.

Fear

Lesson 16

Do not be afraid of sudden fear
Nor of the onslaught of the wicked when it comes;
For the Lord will be your confidence
And will keep your foot from being caught.
Proverbs 3:25-26

What do you fear? (Circle all that apply to you.)

not being accepted not being appreciated bad grades

disappointing Mom or Dad storms getting sick

that someone might die death not being understood

that you won't have any friends being kidnapped the dark

moving dogs that you won't be good enough at something

Other ___________________________________

Fear is the opposite of trust.

Fear comes when we look at the circumstance rather than at God. Think about the life of Jesus' disciple, Peter. Jesus gave to Simon, the son of John, the name "Cephas" or "Peter". "Petros" is Greek for "Rock". Later in Matthew 16:18, Jesus said to Peter, ***"…you are Peter, and upon this rock I will build my church; and the gates of Hades will not overpower it."***

But, we look at his life and wonder why on earth Jesus could call Peter a rock! This is the man that walked on water, but got afraid and sank. This is the man that denied Jesus three times before the rooster crowed when people said that they had seen him with Jesus.

Let's look at these two events a little bit closer.

Matthew 14:24 begins the story of Jesus walking to his disciples on the water. **Read verses 24-26.** In verse 26 you see the disciples' initial reaction to seeing Jesus walking on the waves. They were terrified!! They thought He was a ghost!

Jesus quickly calms them by saying, ***"Take courage, it is I; do not be afraid."*** In other words, Jesus was telling the disciples that **there was no reason to fear because He was**

there. Peter jumped ahead and, demanding truth, seemed fearless as he told Jesus, ***"Lord, if it is You, command me to come to You on the water."*** Jesus said, ***"Come."*** And Peter clamored over the side of the boat to stand on the water with Jesus – no problem - until... Peter took his eyes off of Jesus and looked at the storm all around him. Verse 30 says, ***"But seeing the wind, he became _________________________..."*** That's right! He was fine looking at Jesus, but when he decided to focus on his circumstances, he sank!! Jesus saved him and led him back to the boat.

Write Colossians 3:2 below.

____

____

Now let's look at Peter's denial of Christ. It had been a long night. The disciples had been in the Garden of Gethsemane with Jesus as he prayed. He had taken Peter, James, and John deeper into the garden with Him and asked them to keep watch. They were worn out and fell asleep. But Jesus woke them three times and asked them to stay awake and pray. As Jesus woke them the third time, a troop of soldiers approached. Judas kissed Jesus, identifying Him as the One Who Called Himself Messiah. One of the disciples took a sword and cut off the ear of the slave of the High Priest. Jesus healed the ear and told his disciples to put their swords away. He allowed the soldiers to lead Him out of the garden and into the court of the High Priest.

The disciples were afraid and they fled. All except Peter! He sat outside listening and hoping to find out what was happening. But three times people identified him as having been with Jesus. Three times Peter denied knowing Jesus.

Why do you think that Peter said that he didn't know Jesus? I think he was afraid. Afraid of being taken himself, afraid of being ridiculed for following Jesus, afraid of being told that he was to be cast out of the temple and no longer able to worship there, afraid of Jesus' fate.

In Luke's book about this night, he writes that after Peter had denied Jesus three times when the rooster crowed and then, ***"The Lord turned and looked at Peter...and he went out and wept bitterly."*** (Luke 22:60-62) Do you think that Jesus looked at Peter with rebuke or forgiveness and love? From knowing Jesus and what the Bible says about Him, I have to believe that Jesus was even then, forgiving and loving Peter. But fear kept Peter from being able to accept that gift.

The story does have a happy ending though! Jesus was crucified, buried, and then raised from the dead! Peter ran to the tomb to see if this could be true. He was once again looking for Jesus. Later Peter is out fishing with six other disciples when Jesus shows up on shore. As soon as Peter realized that it was Jesus, **he looked only at Him**, jumped into the lake and swam for His Savior!! We know that Peter kept looking at Jesus even after Jesus was ascended into heaven. He preached about Jesus without fear in Jerusalem and then all around Israel. He was the first disciple to eat with non-Jews, and He eventually was crucified upside down for His beliefs. But, he never turned away in fear again!! He stood as solid as a rock!

Practical Proverbs 

You don't have to live in fear! Matthew 6:33-34 shows us how to live a worry free life.

> ***"But seek first _______________ ________________________________ and His ________________________________, and all these things will be added to you. So do not worry about tomorrow; for tomorrow will care for itself. Each day has enough trouble of its own."***

In other words, keep looking at Jesus, not at your circumstances. Call on Him and He will take care of you. He promises to always be there with us through every circumstance of life! He doesn't take all the bad away, but He gets us through it!

Let's close with this verse from 1 Peter (our hero from today's story), chapter 5 verse 7:

> ***"…casting all your anxiety on Him, because He cares for you."***

When you are in the midst of a scary situation, draw a mental picture of yourself in Jesus' arms. He is there comforting you. Curl up in His lap; look up in His face. Remember that He is on His throne and in charge of everything!!

Next lesson be ready to quote Psalm 1:1-3 to a parent or adult.

The fear of man brings a snare
But he who trusts in the Lord will be exalted.
Proverbs 29:25

Today you are going to make a **"Trust God Box"**. Get a small box, (a kleenex box, an oatmeal box, etc.) and either cut a hole in the bottom that you can reach into or open the bottom up if it is just glued shut. Make a slit in the top or use the opening already there in a Kleenex box. Decorate your box with pictures or material and ribbon or Bible verses. Make it your own!

Now, write down on small slips of papers anything and everything that you are worrying about. Prayerfully put each paper into the box and give that circumstance or person to God. If you start worrying about a situation again, then reach inside your box, take out the paper that you wrote that concern on and pray again giving it back to God. Then replace the paper back into the box. If it is in the box, it is God's problem, not yours!!

After a while, you won't have to keep taking it out and putting it back in again; you will remember that you are not supposed to worry, and you will immediately give it to God! Whenever you think about your situation, thank God that He is handling it.

Remember: **Fear is the opposite of faith and trust.**

Watch Over Your Heart : Media

Lesson 17

Watch over your heart with all diligence,
For from it flows the springs of life.
Proverbs 4:23

How do you "watch over your heart?"

Have you ever heard the old saying, "Input equals output"? Galatians 6:7 puts it this way, ***"...whatever a man sows, this he will also reap."*** Let's think about that for a minute.

- You put gas into a car and out comes energy to drive.
- You put food into your stomach (hopefully nutritious food) and out comes energy to live.
- You put words or commands into a computer and you get out whatever you asked it to do. (Well, you're supposed to get back what you wanted. Sometimes I put in one thing and get something completely unrelated. I almost always learn that I had inputted incorrectly!)
- You put time into training an animal and you get an obedient pet.
- You put time and friendship into a relationship and you get time and friendship back.
- You plant corn and out comes a corn stalk.

You watch over your heart by being careful with what you are putting into your heart!

What do you watch on tv?
What do you listen to on the radio?
What conversations are you involved in with your friends?
What magazines do you read?
What books do you read?

All of these things influence your heart, your thinking, your relationships, and your choices. If you want to make wise choices, then you need to be wise about what you allow into your heart.

Not only do we need to be aware of the content of our media choices, but we also need to be careful how much time we are spending watching, texting, video gaming, etc. Jeff Myers, Ph.D. wrote an article called, "Entertainment-Soaked Culture Damages Kids' Brains". His study reveals that, "The brain was designed in such a way that work and accomplishment stimulate the executive center of the brain, which in turn stimulates the pleasure center of the brain. Work brings satisfaction, and the desire for life satisfaction motivates people to work."

Studies show that kids who play video games, watch tv, listen to music, etc. stimulate the pleasure center without first going through the executive center. In other words, it takes a short cut. The result is effortless pleasure. This means that it becomes, "...**more rewarding to pursue entertainment and less rewarding to accomplish anything of value**." Further results are that academic work becomes harder and less satisfying, social relationships suffer, and logical thought and problem solving become not worth the effort. ADHD and bi-polar disorder have both been linked to an over active pleasure center and an under-active executive center of the brain.

The solution to this is to turn off the tv, radio, i-pod, computer, etc. and get outside and play! Play games, build stuff, have a real conversation, use your imagination to create. Myers says that, "Conversation seems to be a bridge that reconnects the broken-down relationship between the executive and pleasure centers of the brain."

There is a place for media entertainment, but it should be limited and monitored! Talk to your parents about putting healthy limits on technology Once you have limits on the amount of time that you spend on media, you still need to make wise choices on what you watch, play, listen to, etc.

Here are some questions that you should ask yourself about that program, music, or game.

1. Does it support Godly, Biblical life choices? In other words, if the characters are living together outside of marriage, you shouldn't watch it.

2. Is the language uplifting to God. In other words, no cussing or discussing sexually related material.

3. Are the actors, singers, writers, etc..., living a Biblical life? Be careful here, some "Christian" artists sing Christian songs, but do not live their lives according to God's Word.

4. Is the theme in line with Biblical Christianity? Harry Potter books are a problem here. God says in Deuteronomy 18:10-12 that witchcraft is detestable to God.

Not all non-Christian movies, music, etc... are bad – I love "Cars"! But guard your heart and make sure that what you input is glorifying Jesus!

Psalm 101:3 says: ***"I will set no ________________________ thing before my eyes; I hate the work of those who fall away; It shall not fasten its grip on me."***

Television, youtube, music, etc... can fall under this category if it is not wholesome and godly.

Practical Proverbs

Here are some actions that we take to keep our hearts pure and to stay accountable to one another and God.

1. We check out www.pluggedin.com by Focus on the Family to decide what movies, music, television shows, and video games are acceptable. This website tells you the sexual content, language content, violence level, and age levels for popular movies.

2. We keep all computers out in the open areas of our homes and have a filter on each one. (We are all human and subject to temptations). This keeps those temptations at bay!!

3. We only watch television as a family in the living room. No tv's in the bedrooms. We actually watch very little tv and always keep our fingers on the buttons of the remote when we do. We are more likely to watch DVD's of acceptable shows.

4. No R rated movies are allowed in the home, PERIOD!! No exceptions!!

5. TV rarely comes on before 8:00 at night. There's too much other life to live!!

6. The kids in our home know that Mom and Dad always have the right to check texts, Facebook, phone numbers, internet usage, etc. And we do make regular checks on these things.

7. At our house, cell phones were a privilege given at age 17 after getting a driver's license, for emergency purposes. Facebook was not allowed until age 16. Discuss with your Mom and Dad what they think are appropriate ages for these gadgets. I don't recommend them for children under the age of at least 13. Some families will have a family cell phone that can be checked out for an event such as when one member of the family goes to a friend's house.

Can you add any rules or ideas about how you can protect your heart when it comes to media?

____

Okay, you've worked hard! Let's hear it! Quote Psalm 1:1-3 to a parent or adult. Good job!

The good man out of the good treasure of his heart brings forth what is good; and the evil man out of the evil treasure brings forth what is evil; for his mouth speaks from that which fills his heart.
Luke 6:45

Interview the members of your family. Try to question Mom, Dad, siblings, grandparents, aunts, and uncles, if possible. Write down their answers to the following questions.

1. What is your favorite book?

Mom ______________________________
Dad ______________________________
Sibling ______________________________
Sibling ______________________________
Other ______________________________

2. What is your favorite movie?

Mom ______________________________
Dad ______________________________
Sibling ______________________________
Sibling ______________________________
Other ______________________________

3. What is your favorite television show?

Mom ______________________________
Dad ______________________________
Sibling ______________________________
Sibling ______________________________
Other ______________________________

4. What is your favorite magazine?

Mom ______________________________
Dad ______________________________
Sibling ______________________________
Sibling ______________________________
Other ______________________________

5. How do you watch over your heart?

Mom ______________________________
Dad ______________________________

Sibling ____
Sibling ____
Other ____

Do you see any connection to what these people watch and how they act?

____

____

Did you get any good ideas about how to guard your heart?

____

____

Watch Over Your Heart – Relationships

Lesson 18

He who walks with wise men will be wise;
But the companion of fools will suffer harm.
Proverbs 13:20

Whom do you have a relationship with? ______________________________
____

Hopefully you included Mom, Dad, God, sisters, brothers, friends, and other adults in your life – maybe a music teacher or coach, people from your church, etc…

Relationships vary from the closest to casual friends. Take your list of people that you have a relationship with and place each name into the target below with the people that you are closest to in the bull's eye, the next closest in the "20" mark, etc…

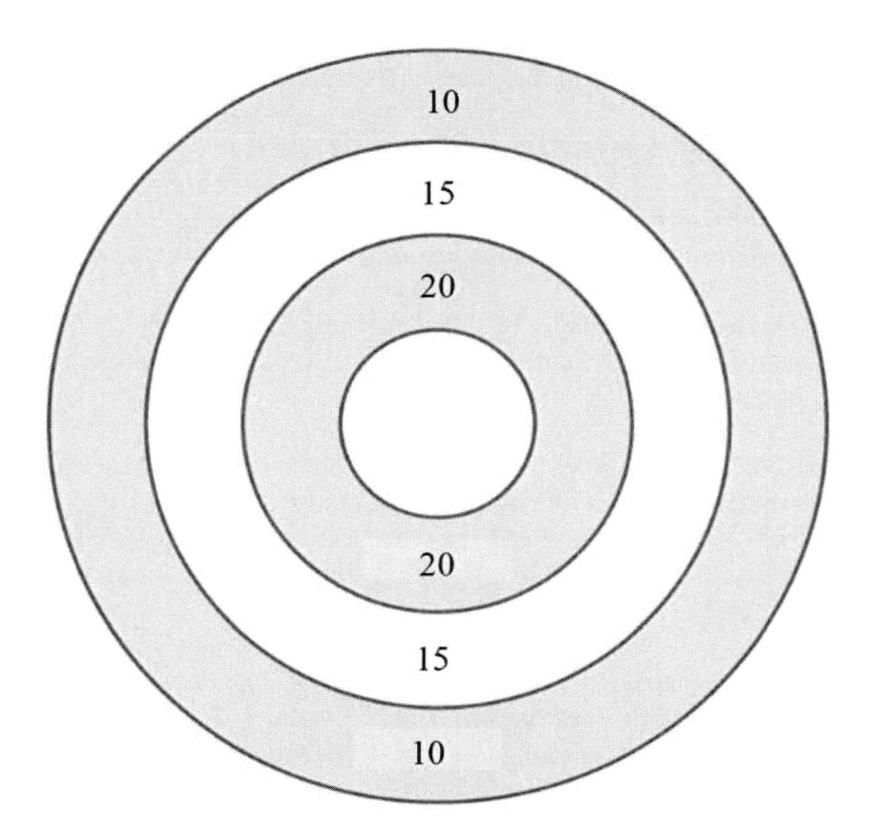

From this diagram you can see that all relationships are not the same!!

Your "bull's eye" people should include Godly Christian people who support you, love you unconditionally, and who believe in you.

The ''20" point level will include those whom you are close to, but that are not as close to you as your bull's eye people. Again, these should be Christians.

Your "15" level people will be those whom you see occasionally, maybe even weekly that you have conversations with, but may not tell your secrets to.

Your "10" people will be those that you see occasionally, maybe even weekly, but you just give a casual hello to.

And then there are those outside of the target that you know and enjoy, but see only occasionally and are on the outside of a personal relationship with you.

As Christians it is important that our closest friends be Christians that can lift us up, pray with and for us, who keep us accountable before God, and who share like values with us.

Yes, we are to have relationships with non-Christians that we might witness to them. But, these should not be our closest friends. "Missionary friendship" or "Missionary dating" almost never works!! This is when you are friends with or date a non-Christian, believing that you will change that person and that they will come to know God.

> 2 Corinthians 6:14-15 says, ***"Do not be bound together with _______________________; for what partnership have righteousness and lawlessness, or what fellowship has light with darkness? Or what harmony has Christ with Belial (Satan), or what has a believer in common with an unbeliever?"***

This unequal partnership is friendship, business partners, marriage partners, etc… We are to love everyone because they were made in the image of God, but we must not be in partnership with unbelievers!!

Your level "5" and "10" people may be unbelievers, but you should keep them at that distance until they become believers. We are to be ready at all times to give an account of the hope that is in us (1 Peter 3:15). Let your words and actions draw unbelievers to ask you questions and be ready to sit with them and explain Jesus to them, but don't make an unbeliever a close friend.

That being said, no one is perfect. Even your "bull's eye" people will make mistakes and let you down. ***"God is mindful that we are but dust!"*** (Psalm 103:14). Don't judge others too harshly; allow for mistakes and repentance; forgive seventy times seven (Matthew 18:21). How is being in relationship "guarding our heart"? I always say that being born again makes us alive, therefore unbelievers are dead in their trespasses and sin (Ephesians 2:1). Dead people will act like dead people!! Yes, some Christians (alive in Christ) also act as if they are dead, but they have a choice; a dead person does not!! Dead people (unbelievers) will

not have the Holy Spirit to convict them of sin, so they don't see anything wrong with sinful behavior. Hang around them too much and you will begin to act just like them.

1 Corinthians 15:33 says: ***"Do not be deceived; 'Bad company __________________ good morals.'"***

Proverbs 4:23 is our next memory verse. Get started!

> **"Watch over your heart with all diligence,**
> **For from it flow the springs of life."**

If we confess our sins,
He is faithful and righteous to forgive us our sins
and to cleanse us from all unrighteousness.
1 John 1:9

There are ups and downs in every relationship. Choosing friends wisely will safeguard your heart. But even godly friends will let you down. Learning to forgive is a huge help in keeping and making friends.

When someone does something that upsets you, what do you say? "He or she __________ me an apology." In other words, you think that there is a debt. To pay that debt your friend must say that he/she is sorry. But, forgiveness is canceling that debt. It is not denying that there was hurt, but choosing to use your will to cancel that debt.

I love Romans 5:8. ***"But God demonstrates His own love toward us, in that while we were yet sinners, Christ died for us."***

Notice that God didn't wait for us to say we were sorry before He took action and chose to forgive us. Jesus' death on the cross was God's forgiveness for everyone before we were even born!! (Note: God's forgiveness is available to everyone, but only by believing and accepting Jesus as Lord and Savior can God's forgiveness be applied to our debt.)

What does Colossians 3:13 say about forgiving others?

> ***"…forgiving each other, whoever has a complaint against anyone; just as the __________________ __________________ _____________, so also should you."***
>
> **How much did Jesus forgive you?** ___________________________________

That's a lot of forgiveness! Remember that even if you have never committed any really bad sins, that all sin breaks the heart of God. To God, pride or lying or rebellion is as much a sin as murder. It is our sin nature that Jesus died to regenerate. Before accepting Jesus as my Lord and Savior, I was guilty – period. Jesus' forgiveness is enough to cover it all!

In Matthew 18:21-22, I don't think that Jesus meant that we were to literally count how many times we have forgiven someone and after the 490th time (70 x 7), we don't have to forgive anymore!! I think that He was saying that His forgiveness was limitless and so should ours be!

Now, I will admit there is a huge gap between deciding to forgive someone and feeling like you have forgiven them or that you even want to be around them again. But, God says to Forgive. This is a choice. The feelings will come along later and you can also keep praying that God will make you feel love for that person again.

Forgiving someone does not mean that you have to get back into a relationship with that person. Sometimes you need to put different boundaries on that relationship. You may need to move that person from your bulls eye to a ring farther out. That's not being unforgiving, that's guarding your heart.

Is there someone that you need to forgive? (Even if they have never or may never say that they are sorry)?

____

Take a minute right now and pray for that person and make the choice to cancel the debt and forgive. Forgiveness is keeping **your** heart pure and clean.

Relationship with God

Lesson 19

I love those who love me;
And those who diligently seek me will find me.
Proverbs 8:17

Proverbs 8:17 is a quote from Wisdom. Wisdom throughout the book of Proverbs is Jesus Christ. Jesus is one of the Trinity. If wisdom loves you, then Jesus loves you, then God loves you!

Often the reason someone won't come to God is because they feel that they have been so bad that God could never forgive them. Was Jesus' death on the cross so weak that it could only cover some sins? Actually, the blood does not cover the sin, but the sinner. **We commit sins because we are sinners.** When we get right with God, He sees us as His righteous ones, pure and beloved. We are cleansed from our sins and are no longer a sinner when we accept Jesus' sacrifice on the cross. If we sin after that, we are already covered!! But, we do need to confess sins because they can keep us from a relationship with God!

Copy 1 John 1:9 ____
____
____
____

Look at Genesis 3:8 What is Adam and Eve's response to God after they sinned?
____

When we sin, we tend to hide. If we lied to Mom, then we hide from Mom. If we took something from Dad and didn't return it, then we hide from Dad. When we sin, we also tend to hide from God. By confessing that sin and putting it out in the open, we can restore our relationship with God. Someone once said that you are only as sick as your sickest secret. If we confess all secrets to God we won't be emotionally or spiritually sick. If we have a physical sickness because of stress or anxiety over unconfessed sin, then that too will be healed! There is much healing in confession.

Read Psalm 32.

This is a confession by David after he committed adultery with Bathsheba. Notice that he first recognizes God's ability to love and forgive. He speaks about his own sinfulness in verse 3 and 4, and his confession in verse 5. In verses 6-7, he rejoices in God's deliverance.

Sin is impurity. If you have a glass of water and put a pinch of dirt in it, it becomes impure. Adding more water will not take the impurity away. Only tossing it all out and starting with

clean water will give you pure water again. We are sinners. Adding good works does not make us pure. Only tossing out the old nature and becoming a new creation will make us pure!! Then for the sake of relationship with God, we need to keep confessing and allowing God to teach us His righteousness.

So **confession is vital to our relationship with God.** Repentance also must take place. To confess is to admit that we have done something wrong, but **repentance is being willing to turn from that sin and never commit it again.** ***"God is mindful that we are but dust"*** (Ps. 103:14) and will forgive us over and over again, but constant sin erodes our relationship with God. We must want and desire to repent. God will then give us the power to repent.

Read 1 Corinthians 10:13

"No temptation has overtaken you but such is common to man; and God is ___________, who will not allow you to be tempted beyond what you are able, but with the temptation will ____________________ the way of escape also, so that you will be able to endure it."

Temptations will come. Remember that being tempted is not a sin, but dwelling on that temptation is and will lead you to act out. When you are tempted, pray that God will give you the strength to overcome it and a way to escape it. Sometimes escape is physically removing your body from the temptation – leave the room, turn off the tv, walk away. Sometimes it is a mental escape – think different thoughts, dwell on God, talk about other things, read a different book, call someone. Satan is the accuser and the tempter. The battle is in the mind, and you must take every thought captive and pray.

Work on your memory verse Proverbs 4:23.

"Watch over your _____________ with all ___________________,
For from it _________________ the ________________ _____ ___________."

I am the vine, you are the branches;
he who abides in Me and I in him,
he bears much fruit,
for apart from Me you can do nothing.
John 15:5

A key to overcoming temptation is "to abide". Draw a picture of your house.

Your house is where you abide, live, dwell, and spend your time. The Bible says that we are to abide in God's Word, in Jesus, and in God. That is where we are to spend our thoughts. We can live this life with our bodies, but we are to always be in the presence of God!

Read through John 15:1-11.

How many times do you see the word abide? ________________

Now read 1 John 2:5, 14, 24, 27-28 and 3:24, 4:12-16.

Abiding seems to be a big deal to God. So, how do we abide?

Philippians 4:8 says that we are dwell on ***"…whatever is true, whatever is pure, whatever is lovely, whatever is of good repute, if there is any excellence and if anything worthy of praise…"***

God's Word, Jesus, and God Himself are all of these things!! We are to think about and dwell on these things. When we see life's circumstances through God's eyes and trust in Him to make all things work for our good (Romans 8:28), then we are dwelling on Him. When we sing praises to God in spite of our circumstances and thank Him for each circumstance, then we are dwelling or abiding in Him. Reading God's Word and putting it into our heart is dwelling on God.

Below write ways that you can dwell on God.

1. Remember that God is in every circumstance
2.
3.
4.
5.

A monk from the 1700's said that abiding with God is "Practicing the Presence of God". He wrote a book by that title. If we are abiding in God, then we are aware of His constant presence and that is where great joy is found no matter what the circumstances are!

Romans 12:2 says that we are to ***"... be ______________________ by the renewing of your mind..."*** That renewing takes place as we put God's Word into our hearts!

Colossians 3:1 is a key verse for believers. Write this verse below.

____

____

____

When we keep our minds on things above, then we put the things here on earth in proper perspective. Eternal concerns should outweigh temporary, earthly concerns, although we tend to get it the other way around! When you feel anxious, go to Jesus, abide in His Word and His promises. Walk in the garden with Him, sit with Him, or dance with Him! Visualizing yourself with Jesus and then talking to Him will help you to abide.

Relationships with Siblings and Friends

Lesson 20

"Behold, how good and how pleasant it is
For brothers to dwell together in unity…"
Psalm 133:1

If you have brothers or sisters you know that you don't always get along. This is true about friends, too. So what should these relationships look like?

Write out Romans 12:18

____

____

____

Well, are you doing all that you can do to live at peace with your brothers or sisters? At our house we have an overriding rule. If our house rules don't address a situation then the rule is: **Is it making the other person feel special?** If not, then you are in the wrong. Are your words and actions making your brothers or sisters feel special?

Home needs to be a safe place. Outside those walls is the world and it can be a cruel, unforgiving place. Let others put people down and be sarcastic and be mean-spirited, but within the walls of your house do all you can to "… be at peace with all men."

That means honoring your parents and honoring your siblings even when they are not acting honorable. Hopefully, they will extend grace in your direction in time of need also!!

Let's see what Jesus says about His brothers. Keep in mind that this is more about adult relationships than children within the home. But, it can help us get some perspective. In Matthew 12:46-48, Jesus was speaking to a crowd while His mother and brothers were outside wanting to talk to Him. When someone told Jesus that they were outside waiting on Him, He replied, ***"Who is My mother and who are My brothers?"*** Reaching out His hand toward His disciples, He said ***"Behold My mother and My brothers! For whoever does the will of My Father who is in heaven, he is My brother and sister and mother."*** Jesus was not dishonoring His mom and brothers here, but teaching to make a point. Later on at the cross, Jesus fulfills His responsibility to His mother, by asking John to take care of her, and we know some of His earthly brothers became pillars in the first church.

Jesus was saying that when we are born again and have chosen to do God's will, then we have entered into a new family – a heavenly family called "The Church". This Church is the body of all born again believers. God is the Father, Jesus is the first born, our Big Brother. We are to treat other believers as we would treat our own earthly family. God would have us to talk and act in love, to not argue or fight, to not be jealous but rather be content. If we can

learn to act this way in our earthly home with our parents and siblings, then we will be able to act and react appropriately to the Church as adults. **Home is just a training ground.**

If your parents and siblings are believers, then you have a double duty to love and respect them. If they are not, then you must, by your behavior, be an example of God's love that they might know Him.

Draw a picture of your family (Stick figures are okay!)

Under each family member write either believer or unbeliever. Then begin to pray how you can love each one of them with God's love.

Be ready to say Proverbs 4:23 to a parent or adult during the next lesson.

Lesson 20 Worksheet

Little children, let us not love with word or with tongue,
but in deed and truth.
1 John 3:18

List 5 things that you appreciate about your Dad:
1.
2.
3.
4.
5.

List 5 things that you appreciate about your Mom:
1.
2.
3.
4.
5.

List 5 things you appreciate about your brother or sister: (If you have more than one sibling write 5 things about each on the back of this paper.)
1.
2.
3.
4.
5.

List 5 things that you do to encourage your family daily:
1.
2.
3.
4.
5.

If you cannot think of 5 things that you do to encourage your family, write down some ideas that you could begin to do. Examples: Ask Mom if you can help with dinner or cleanup, say something nice to everyone every day, play with your younger sibling so Mom and Dad can have a break, etc... Ask God to give you some ideas and to make you mindful of things that you can do.

Relationship with Parents

Lesson 21

A wise son makes a father glad,
But a foolish son is a grief to his mother.
Proverbs 10:1

The roles of Father, Mother, Son, and Daughter are very important to God. He calls Himself our Father. What do you think He means or is implying by referring to Himself as our Father?

____

____

A father is supposed to protect and provide for his family. He is to be the teacher of God to his children. He is to be the leader of the home. Your Mom is supposed to comfort you, nourish you, teach you, and love you. Your Mom and Dad may or may not fulfill their duties, but God says that the children are to honor their parents. He does not say to honor them when you get your way or honor them when they do something right. No, He just says to honor them. So, what is honor? And how do I honor my parents?

To honor someone is to hold them in high esteem or high respect. God gave us moms and dads to be His representatives here on earth. So, when you respect or honor your parents, you are respecting and honoring God! When you are obeying your parents, you are obeying God.

Are your parents perfect? No!! But do they love you and try to make wise decisions for you and the rest of the family? Probably! You can honor your parents by accepting that they, too, are human and make mistakes. Extend them some grace and forgiveness. If you have a parent that is truly not doing things worthy of respect – such as abuse or drugs or yelling, etc., you can still honor the fact that they are your parents and that God has placed them into your life. Be honoring anyway and God will honor your heart attitude. At the very least, commit never to speak badly of your parents and be ready and willing to take care of them if they cannot take care of themselves.

Let's see what the Proverbs says about our parents. Look up these verses and write how you *should* or *should not* behave with your parents.

Proverbs 15:20 ____

Proverbs 19:26 ____

Proverbs 20:20 ____

Practical Proverbs 

Proverbs 23:22 ____

Proverbs 23:25____

Proverbs 28:24 ____

Proverbs 29:15 ____

Proverbs 30:11 ____

Proverbs 30:17 ____

Remember that your Mom and Dad make choices for you and the family the best they know how. Hopefully they are Christians and can lead in God's way, but even if they are not, God can use them to lead you. Trust God and obey your parents.

Is there ever a time when you should go against what your parents tell you? Only with much prayer and godly counsel and only if your parents ask you to do something that goes against God's commands. If so, then speak to a godly person and see if they will go with you to respectfully talk with your parents.

However, most differences with your parents are over something quite insignificant – curfew, activities, entertainment choices, friends, etc. Even though it will be hard, give Mom and Dad the benefit of the doubt and watch God work in the midst of the disagreement.

I wanted to go to a particular college. My parents wanted me to go to a different school. I followed their lead. During my first year of college, my parents moved out of state. After my freshman year I joined them and there was a college in their new town. It was just the kind of college that I had wanted to attend! I met my husband there and the rest is history!! If I had argued and insisted, then my life would have played out much differently. God knew who and when and how. By honoring my parents, God worked out His plan.

Respect Mom and Dad. That is the only commandment given by God that comes with a promise. Read Deuteronomy 5:16 and write what that promise is. ____________________

____

Be sure to tell a parent or an adult your memory verse: Proverbs 4:23.

See if you can also remember the definition of wisdom: Wisdom is…

If you are really working hard, you can quote Proverbs 3:3-6 and Psalm 1:1-3 also!!

Children, obey your parents in the Lord,
for this is right.
Ephesians 6:1

For each letter of the word OBEDIENCE, write a heart attitude that you should have when obeying your parents or something that you can do to obey your parents. I did the first one for you.

Observe what needs to be done and do it with a cheerful heart.

B

E

D

I

E

N

C

E

Contentment

Lesson 22

But godliness actually is a means of great gain
when accompanied by contentment.
1 Timothy 6:6

Even though the words "content" or "contentment" are not actually found in the book of Proverbs, it is still an underlying theme to the book. If a man walks in integrity, righteousness, and wisdom, then he will find contentment.

So what is contentment? ____

What makes you content? ____

Contentment is the state of being satisfied. That could be a physical satisfaction which you might feel after eating your favorite meal and dessert. Or it could me a mental contentment of knowing that you did well on your last science test. Or it could be a spiritual fulfillment of walking with Jesus and being at peace.

Let's see what Paul, the Great Disciple of the New Testament, had to say about contentment. First, let us look at Paul's life up to this point. He had it all! Heritage, education, opportunities, etc… then He gave it all up to live for Jesus! In doing so he lost his eyesight and even though God miraculously healed his eyes, we see evidence throughout his writing that he struggled with his eyesight for the rest of his life. Yet, even living for Jesus, Paul faced a lot of hardships.

Read 2 Corinthians 11:23-33. List the many different trials Paul endured. I found 20.

1.	8.	15.
2.	9.	16.
3.	10.	17.
4.	11.	18.
5.	12.	19.
6.	13.	20.
7.	14.	

Now, if I had been through all of that, I might be a little bit grumpy!! I might argue with God and wonder why He is letting His child go through all of these torments. But listen to Paul's words: Philippians 4:11 – ***"Not that I speak from want, for I have learned to be content in whatever circumstances I am."*** Wow!! Those are words from someone who really has learned to trust in God.

A great preacher, Charles Spurgeon, once said, **"When you can't see God's Hand, trust His heart."** We know God's heart towards us (we are His beloved children). So learning to be content in whatever He has allowed into our lives is simply trusting that He is sovereign and loves us and wants what is best for us in the long run. To do that we must have an eternal perspective. But, we like to be fulfilled and satisfied **NOW!**

God says through Paul in 2 Corinthians 4:17:

> ***"For momentary, light affliction is producing for us an eternal weight of glory far beyond all comparison, while we look not at the things which are _________________, but at the things which are ___________ seen; for the things which are seen are temporal, but the things which are not seen are eternal."***

What do you tend to look at? The temporary things of the NOW or the eternal things of God? ____

Pray that God will give you the heart to desire eternal things and the wisdom to know what those things are.

Here is a hint to what eternal things are:

What eternal treasure is not: ____________________________

Matthew 6:19-21
Matthew 19:21
James 5:1-3

What eternal treasure is: ________________________________

2 Corinthians 4:6-7
Galatians 5:22-23

Our new memory verse is Proverbs 14:12.

> **"There is a way which seems right to a man,**
> **But its end is the way of death."**

Get started!!

This is the message we have heard from Him and announce to you,
that God is Light,
and in Him there is no darkness at all.
1 John 1:5

You are going to lead your family in Bible time today. Make sure you read through the entire lesson and make preparations ahead of time.

Start by setting up an obstacle course around a room in your house. Then turn off all of the lights (if that makes the room dark enough that you really ***can't*** see anything) or blindfold each person in turn. Only let one person into the room at a time so they can't peek. Stand at the other side of the room and ask them to come to you. Keep very still and don't let anyone help them. They should bang around a bit, stumble into things, and generally get frustrated.

Once everyone has had a turn, turn on the light or take off the blindfolds. Let everyone study the obstacle course and get an idea where everything is at. Then ask them to walk through it. This should be no problem.

Next, put the blindfolds back on or turn off the light again. Again have everyone go through the obstacles.

Once more with the lights off or the blindfolds on, everyone needs to go through the obstacles, but this time you lead each one through by holding their hand and speaking encouragement and instruction.

Then turn the lights on, take off the blindfolds, and get ready for discussion.

Q. How did you feel when you had to go through the obstacles and you couldn't see?

Q. Was it easier to do the obstacle course in the light?

Q. What made it easier to go through the obstacle course in the dark the second time rather than the first time in the dark?

Q. How did having someone guide you help you to get through the obstacles?

Say: I learned today about a famous preacher, Charles Spurgeon. He said, **"When you can't see God's hand, trust His heart."**

Q. What does this saying have to do with our obstacle course?
(A. When we knew what was there, we could trust what we knew and get through it easier. When someone who knew the path led us through, it was easier. When we know God, we can trust Him to lead us through the dark. He never changes, so what we know in the light, we can trust in the dark.)

Q. How important then is it to get to know God while everything is going well?

Q. How does knowing God and trusting God through the tough times, help us to be content? (A. We can focus on His character, His plans, His promises, and know that He is right there with us and has a purpose for everything that we are going through.)

Say: Author and theologian, Ian Maclaren, said**, "Those who know the path to God can find it in the dark."**

Contentment comes when we can trust in God's wisdom, power, love, and guidance even when we are not *feeling* it.

Pray: God thank you that we can trust that You are the same in the dark times as You are in the good times. Thank you for watching over us, preparing us for this life, and going with us through it. Teach me to encourage others through their dark times. Help me to know You more and more and make me at peace and content because You are my God. Amen

Money

Lesson 23

The refining pot is for silver and the furnace for gold,
But the Lord tests hearts.
Proverbs 17:3

You will notice in Proverbs 17:3, above, that there is a place for money – the pot and the furnace. The pot and the furnace were used to purify the precious metals from the rock and other substances that surrounded it. By heating it up, the gold or silver would liquefy and drop to the bottom and then impurities would float to the top where they would then be scraped off. So the pot and the furnace was a place to purify metals that the Old Testament cultures would then turn into coins.

Just as the gold and silver would be purified, God is concerned with us having a pure heart. He allows us to go through the fire sometimes in order to purify our hearts. It is only when we have been through a difficult time and seen God's faithfulness and protection and provision, that our faith grows and we know that He will always be there for us, because we have experienced it!!

Money is spoken of a lot in the Old Testament as well as the New Testament. Jesus told more parables about money than anything else. So, can a godly man have money and riches? Can a rich man be godly? What is the relationship between having money and having God? We will look at quite a few verses to sort this all out. Right now we will get to the bottom line.

Turn to Matthew 6:24. Fill in the blanks for this verse.

> "***No one can serve two _________________________; for either he will hate the one and love the other, or he will be devoted to one and despise the other. You cannot serve God and _______________________."***

This verse **does not** say that we shouldn't have money. It **does** say that Christians shouldn't serve money. In other words, money can't be what our life is about. It can't be what we strive for and dream about. It can't be the most important thing in our life. When making money becomes too important it becomes a god in our lives, an idol. And God has already told us that He is a jealous God and doesn't want us to serve or worship any other god, except Him (Commandments 1, 2, and 3 - Deuteronomy 5:7-9). Desiring things that someone else has and we don't have is coveting (Commandment 10 – Deuteronomy 5:21).

Jesus even said that it is easier for a camel to go through the eye of a needle than for a rich man to go to heaven (Matthew 19:24). In Jerusalem, at that time, there was a gate that was so small, it was compared to the eye of a needle. A camel could get through it, but the beast would have to go down on his knees and struggle to get through. So it was not impossible, but very difficult for a camel to go through the eye of a needle. In the same way, it is very difficult, but not impossible, for a rich man to go to heaven. Why is this? God knows our hearts. Remember the verse at the beginning of this lesson: Proverbs 17:3? ***"But the Lord tests ________________."***

It is a rare man that can be rich and still serve only God. The more we have, the more consumed we tend to become in keeping our things nice, in good repair, protected, used in ways that will benefit us, etc... For example, our family lives modestly. My husband provides well for us, but not extravagantly. We don't have a pool, therefore we don't need a high fence. We don't have expensive paintings or jewelry, so we don't have an alarm system or guards. We don't own thousands of acres, so we don't need a helicopter or farm equipment. We buy simple clothes and don't need to spend our time shopping, trying on and accessorizing. You get the picture. Write an example of one thing that you have or do that requires a second thing that you need to have. Because I have ______________________, I also need to have ______________________. Life can get complicated!!

There are godly men that God has given much wealth to that they might use their abundance for the Lord. R. G. Letourneau who started and owned Letourneau Technologies and also founded Letourneau University, and the Mayo brothers who started the Mayo Clinics all used their abundance for God's kingdom by giving away 1/2 or more of the millions that they made. They sponsored missionaries, Christian schools, churches, etc. They did not consider their fortune for their own use, but rather for the kingdom of God.

Unfortunately, most of mankind uses their wealth for their own pleasures. I am sure this is why God asks that we tithe, or give, 1/10 of everything that we make to the church. Tithing is a way of acknowledging that everything we have is God's. We can also give above the tithe and just use our resources to bless God. That shows a heart of trust and love, of devotion and faithfulness. When you receive a gift or a wage, remember God first and then be thankful that He has provided the rest for you to use to take care of yourself and family. When it comes to money, God wants us to have a heart of contentment and trust and thankfulness.

Practice your memory verse: Proverbs 14:12.

"There is a ______________ which seems ___________ to a __________,
But its ___________ is the way of _______________."

**A good name is to be more desired than great wealth,
Favor is better than silver and gold.
Proverbs 22:1**

If you had a million dollars, how would you use it?

____

____

If you had a thousand dollars, how would you use it?

____

____

If you had a hundred dollars, how would you use it?

____

____

If you had ten dollars, how would you use it?

____

____

List 20 things that you are thankful for:

1.
2.
3.
4.
5.
6.
7.
8.
9.
10.
11.
12.
13.
14.
15.
16.
17.
18.
19.
20.

Read Hebrews 13:5 and fill in the blanks.

"Make sure that your character is free from the love of ______________________, being ______________________ with what you have; for He Himself has said, 'I will never desert you, nor will I ever forsake you…'"

Two things I asked of You,
Do not refuse me before I die;
Keep deception and lies far from me,
Give me neither poverty nor riches;
Feed me with the food that is my portion,
That I not be full and deny You and say, "Who is the Lord?"
Or that I not be in want and steal,
And profane the name of my God.
Proverbs 30:7-9

Look up the following verses in Proverbs and see what God has to say about money. Read what God's Word says and then rephrase it in your own words. I did the first one for you.

Proverbs 10:15 ***"The rich man's wealth is his fortress…"*** ____________ A rich man trusts in his money to protect ____________

Proverbs 10:22 ***"It is the blessing of the Lord that makes rich, And He adds no sorrow to it."*** ____________

Proverbs 11:4 ***"Riches do not profit in the day of wrath…"*** ____________

____

Proverbs 11:28 ***"He who trusts in his riches will fall…"*** ____________

____

Proverbs 13:25 ***"The righteous have enough to satisfy his appetite…"*** ____________

____

Proverbs 15:16 ***"Better is a little with the fear of the Lord than great treasure and turmoil with it."*** ____________

Proverbs 18:11 ***"A rich man's wealth is his strong city, And like a high wall in his own imagination."*** ____________

Proverbs 22:9 ***"He who is generous will be blessed…"*** ____________

____

Proverbs 28:6 ***"Better is the poor who walks in his integrity than he who is crooked though he be rich."*** ____________

Proverbs 28:11 ***"The rich man is wise in his own eyes…"*** ____________

____

Proverbs 30:7-10 is a good prayer for each of us. **Read it.** This is a good definition of contentment!!

Attitudes

Lesson 24

The foolishness of man ruins his way,
And his heart rages against the Lord.
Proverbs 19:3

It's all in the attitude! Mary Poppins sang a song, "Just a spoonful of sugar makes the medicine go down, the medicine go down, the medicine go down. Just a spoonful of sugar makes the medicine go down in the most delightful way."

That spoonful of sugar is your outlook or attitude.

When you are asked to do a task that you either don't like doing or would rather not do at the moment, what is your attitude?

Circle one: angry frustrated joyful bothered glad

resentful lazy unappreciated happy

disgusted jealous unloved overwhelmed

What is your attitude or reaction when someone wrongs you?

Circle one: angry resentful joyous peaceful pity

depressed rejected misunderstood sympathetic

Your attitude is a choice!

That's right, just because you have always acted that way before, doesn't mean that you have to continue to act or react that way this time or the next time. You can choose to act in a way that will please God. I grew up with a mom who was depressed. That is how she responded to the circumstances of her life. I grew up thinking that was the way to respond. But when I realized that I didn't have to respond with depression, I broke free and chose constructive conversation and happiness instead!! I also grew up in a home where there was a lot of yelling. I found myself yelling at my kids, too. I prayed that God would take the anger out of my heart so that I could respond with compassion and patience. He told me that I was praying wrong. He said that I should pray, "God fill me up with so much of You that there will be no room for this anger." I began to read the Bible more, praise God more, and pray more. Pretty soon, I noticed a difference. And now, years later, I rarely, if ever, yell!

So why did God give us emotions, good and bad? Let's look a little bit at God's character.

Read the following verses and write the attitude or emotion that God had in that situation.

Exodus 4:14 ______________________

Exodus 34:14 ____________________

Deuteronomy 13:17 (this one has three) ___________________, ________________,
____

Isaiah 63:7 (this one has three also) ______________________, _________________,
____

1 John 4:16 _______________________

We were made in the image of God. God was angry, jealous, loving, kind, good, etc… So, as His image, we, too, experience these emotions.

No emotion is "bad". In Ephesians 4:26 we are told to ***"…be angry and yet do not sin; do not let the sun go down on your anger, and do not give the devil an opportunity."*** We are not told not to be angry, but with that anger, we should not sin. **Anger is a detection signal**. It tells us that our needs for love, affection, worth, or affirmation are not being met. So, when we become angry the first thing that we should do is ask ourselves "Why am I angry?" When you can identify the source of your anger, then you can talk with the person that made you angry, or another trusted person, and explain why the situation made you angry. Let's look at some examples.

You wake up in the morning and realize that your brother or sister borrowed your favorite sweater or toy. You are angry. Why? You probably feel that they didn't value you enough to ask permission to borrow the item. Instead of going to them yelling and screaming you could say to them, "I noticed that you borrowed my sweater (or toy). It makes me angry that you didn't value me enough to ask my permission to use it. Next time, please ask before you take something of mine."

The key here is to approach other people respectfully and calmly. If they cannot be respectful and calm, then give them some time and try again. Another suggestion is to use "I statements". Rather than saying, "You did this or that," say: "I feel (angry, hurt, frustrated, confused, etc…)." This keeps the other person from feeling attacked and they won't get so defensive. It takes humility on your part, but it is well worth learning to communicate this way. Learning to communicate effectively is hard work, but will pay off in all your relationships for the rest of your life.

There is a godly anger. We should be angry when we see evil. We should be angry when we witness sin. That anger should lead us to positive action, either sharing the gospel with someone or taking part in stopping the evil. Missionaries were key to stopping the Chinese practice of binding young girls' feet. Binding broke their bones and left them crippled so that they might have small and dainty feet for their husbands to be. Missionaries also stopped the practice in India of sati, the burning of the wife when the husband died. Anger at injustice should move you to action.

Jealousy is usually caused by discontentment with what we have compared to what someone else has. When we are grateful to God for everything that He has blessed us with, then we won't need to be jealous.

But there is another type of jealousy – a godly jealousy. This is the jealousy of wanting a right relationship with someone that you love. God was jealous for Israel, because they were rightfully His children, but they chose to worship something else (idols). God is jealous when a Christian chooses to worship something besides Him. A man will experience godly jealousy if his wife decides to leave him and marry another man. A daughter who does not have a relationship with her mother because of abuse, will feel a godly jealousy if she sees her mom trying to "mother" someone else.

All emotions are neutral and can be used for good or evil – even love. If you use love to manipulate someone or offer conditional love based upon their performance, than it is not a godly love. Godly love is unconditional.

Our next lesson will look more closely at anger and the proper ways to show anger.

Be ready to tell your memory verse to a parent or adult during the next lesson! You should be able to say: Proverbs 14:12
Proverbs 4:23
Proverbs 3:5-6
Psalm 1:1-3

"Whatever you do, do your work heartily,
as for the Lord rather than for men."
Colossians 3:23

Write Colossians 3:17 ____
____
____

I don't like to clean bathrooms, but it comes with the territory of being a mom! When I clean toilets I thank God that we have indoor plumbing! I sing praises to him for our home. This gets my mind off the yuck of the task and helps me to refocus on what is important – God and the people in the house.

What tasks or chores are you expected to do that you really don't like? ________
____

Next time that you have to do this chore, take a spoonful of sugar (sing or pray praises to God) and see if the job doesn't get done faster and with a good attitude. **Attitude is a choice!!** Make wise choices and they will become habits.

Read Proverbs 21:19 and Proverbs 27:15. **What bad attitude did the woman in these verses have?** She was ______________________________.

Don't think that only girls can be contentious. Look up Proverbs 26:21. Men can be contentious as well.

Look up the word contention in a dictionary and write the definition here:
____
____

Someone who is contentious starts arguments, loves to dispute and cause controversy.

Do you tend to be contentious? ________

Know this: the attitude of the mom and dad sets the tone for the family. When my husband and I approach difficulty with joy and diligence, my children do not bicker and fight. When we wake up on the wrong side of the bed, it seems everyone else does, too! You are not the mom or dad yet, but getting in the habit of choosing a joyful attitude can never start too young!! Try smiling even when you don't feel like it. Try praising God for the sunshine when everything seems to be going wrong. Sing a song of praise when you would rather pout! It will turn your day around!!

**But the fruit of the Spirit is love, joy, peace, patience,
kindness, goodness, faithfulness, gentleness,
self-control; against such things there is no law.
Galatians 5:22-23**

Draw a train engine pulling one car.

Now write "emotions" on the engine and "Truth of God's Word" on the car. Make your track ahead of the train broken and dangerous. This is what happens when we let our emotions steer us. We make bad decisions; we speak out of anger or frustration. But we don't speak and practice God's truth.

Now draw the same train engine and car, but write "emotions" on the car and "Truth of God's Word" on the engine. This time your tracks should be straight and sturdy!!

When we remember God's truths and allow those to lead our choices and decisions rather than our emotions, then our emotions will eventually get on board and follow along. Forgiveness is a choice. If we willfully choose to forgive someone, we may not feel forgiving towards them right away. But through prayer and praise, God will bring a peace and forgiving feeling into your heart.

Anger

Lesson 25

He who is slow to anger has great understanding,
But he who is quick-tempered exalts folly.
Proverbs 14:29

What makes you angry? ____

Are you pretty laid back or are you quick-tempered? ________________________

Do others hurt your feelings easily? ______________________________

Anger is not bad, in and of itself. Anger is actually healthy. God made our emotions, remember? We get angry when some basic needs are not met. **Those needs are love and affirmation** (affirmation is given when someone says or does something for us that makes us feel worthy). When we don't feel loved or affirmed then we get angry or hurt. Hurt is just anger that won't come out of hiding! Anger is not a sin. Ephesians 4:26, says **"Be angry, but sin not."** The sin comes in when we act out our anger in hurtful ways or when we dwell on thoughts that are not God's truths – rebellion or revenge.

If anger is not a sin, then what is it? **Anger is a warning signal that something is wrong.** I am not feeling loved or affirmed. I can discuss my feelings in a productive way or I can scream and yell and kick things and get into trouble! I have a choice. **You have a choice.** Learning to talk things out with someone can take some practice, but it is always the right way to handle anger. If you can't have a conversation with the person who made you mad, then find someone who can listen and be calm and not get rattled themselves (usually an adult). Be careful not to become a gossip, just telling to tell. You talk about your anger in order to understand the other person or situation, to process the emotions so that you can think in a godly way, and to sort out the best action to take.

Abortion makes me angry, but I do not bomb abortion clinics. I help at a pregnancy help center and encourage young moms and train them in God's words.

I get angry at myself when I cook something and it comes out of the oven all gooey and icky. I don't listen to Satan's lies about my being a bad person who can't do anything right. Instead, I laugh, tell my husband, and order a pizza!

Write about a time that you were angry and let it all hang out. What were the results?

Practical Proverbs

Write about a time that you were angry and handled it by talking it out with someone. What were the results?

Some people (me!) need to have a physical release of emotional energy before I can talk things out. There are healthy ways to do this such as running, shooting baskets, beating your pillow, etc. And there are unhealthy ways of getting anger out physically such as hitting, kicking, yelling, etc...

What healthy way can you physically release your angry emotions? ____________________

You might need to discuss this with a parent and ask them if they think your choice is acceptable to them.

What unhealthy way of releasing angry emotions have you used in the past? _____________

Remember – **It is a choice!** Choose wisely!

There are healthy ways and unhealthy ways to communicate. Unhealthy communication seeks to hurt the other person, doesn't listen to the other's viewpoint, is condemning, holds grudges, and is stubborn, immovable, and demanding.

Healthy communication seeks to listen to all viewpoints, tries to understand, is willing to seek alternatives, cares about the other person, and is able to forgive.

When we don't forgive or we hold onto our anger, then that anger can turn into bitterness. **Bitterness is like drinking poison and hoping the other person will die from it**!! It will turn your insides upside down and can cause headaches, depression, thoughts of revenge, or thoughts of suicide.

Hebrews 12:15 says ***"See to it that no one comes short of the grace of God; that no root of bitterness springing up causes you trouble, and by it many be defiled…"***

Bitterness comes from anger, hurt, or unforgiveness. Uproot bitterness before it gets a strong hold. It's easier and less painful to deal with it *before* it gets embedded into your heart.

Quote your memory verse to a parent or an adult. Proverbs 14:12.

**Brethren, even if anyone is caught in any trespass,
you who are spiritual, restore such a one in a spirit of gentleness;
each one looking to yourself, so that you too will not be tempted.
Galatians 6:1**

Place these phrases in the correct column.

Tries to understand

Hurts the other person

Is condemning

Listens to all viewpoints

Is willing to seek alternatives

Holds grudges

Is able to forgive

Is self-seeking

Cares about the other

Is stubborn, immovable, and demanding

Unhealthy Communications

Healthy Communication

Love

Lesson 26

Better is a dish of vegetables where love is
Than a fatted ox served with hatred.
Proverbs 15:17

Perhaps someday you will "fall in love" and get married. So what exactly is love and if it is so wonderful, how come there is so much divorce? Can love last? What if I don't love the person I married anymore?

These are all great questions and the answers all rely on the definition of "love". Love is not an emotion. **Love is a commitment and duty**. Hopefully you will feel some emotional love for your spouse, but there will be plenty of times that you may not even like your spouse. By sacrificing and acting in a loving way, those feelings will return. Let's look at God's definition of love.

John 3:16 ***"For God so loved the world, that He gave His one and only son…"***

God's love manifested itself into action. Love is giving! That's right love is not about getting your needs met, or making sure that you feel good; love is concerned about the other person to the point of sacrifice. My husband loves me so much that when I have surgery (I have had 7 surgeries), he sacrifices his time and his pleasures to stay by my side, make me meals, and even do the laundry!! I love him so much that I watch action movies with him even though I would rather watch a princess movie.

Notice that love is about giving. It sure takes a lot of self-control to love someone forever!! Love comes with maturity as a Christian. A marriage based on emotional love **will not last**. In a godly marriage, divorce is not an option. If we have a problem, we better fix it because neither one of us is leaving!! Most marital problems stem from sin - selfishness, pride, fear, etc… To keep a healthy marriage, both partners must have a growing relationship with God.

Marriage is not for a person who is unsure of himself and empty inside and emotionally needy. **A person cannot fill that void; only God can**. Rather a person is ready to become a wife or husband when they are content with themselves before God. In marriage, ½ and ½ don't make a whole; rather a whole and a whole make a great marriage.

That's all good, but what about now! You are not old enough to get married. Well, the Bible gives us guidelines on how we should treat other young men and women.

Read 1 Timothy 5:1-2.

How should we treat young men? ____

How should we treat young women? ________________________________

The world says that boys and girls should start dating as young as 6th and 7th grade. This only leads to trouble. Young boys and girls are not emotionally or spiritually ready to handle that kind of relationship. Boys and girls that date early will also tend to push the acceptable physical limits in their relationships. God made our bodies to respond to our spouses in a particular way so that we might have children and find pleasure with one another in marriage. If you start "just holding hands", that will trigger your body and emotions into wanting more. So then you kiss. Then you start touching... Studies show that a couple that lives together before marriage is 60% more likely to get a divorce than a couple that waits until the wedding night to have sex.

On the line below draw a vertical line where you think that childhood ends and adulthood begins.

birth____**death**
0 **35** **70**

You have all of your life to be an adult and to take on adult responsibilities and relationships. Enjoy your childhood! Be active, have fun friends, play a sport, play an instrument, help out around the house, play board games. Be a kid!!

God knows when and who will be your mate. Trust in Him to guide and lead; leave the boy/girl flirtations until you are an adult. **Now is the time to work on becoming the person that someone would want to marry some day!** In choosing friends, watch how that person responds to their authorities: do they respect their Mom and Dad? Do they listen and obey teachers? This will give you a big hint into their character.

What is character? Abraham Lincoln says that, **"Character is like a tree and reputation like a shadow. The shadow is what we think of it; the tree is the real thing."**

Dwight L. Moody, a famous preacher, said, **"Character is what you are in the dark."**

Who are you in the dark?

Our new memory verse is Proverbs 21:23.

"He who guards his mouth and his tongue,
Guards his soul from troubles."

In this is love, not that we loved God,
but that He loved us
and sent His Son to be the propitiation for our sins.
I John 4:10

"Propitiation" is the payment for something. Jesus' blood paid the price for our sins. He appeased a holy God that could not have a relationship with sinners. We deserved death, but He paid that we might have life. All because of His great love for us.

Married love is a commitment for life. Let's look at the "Love Chapter" and see what else we can learn about love. Turn to 1 Corinthians chapter 13. Fill in the blanks.

1 *"If I speak with the tongues of men and of angels, but do not have __________, I have become a noisy gong or a clanging cymbal.*
2 *If I have the gift of prophecy, and know all mysteries and all knowledge; and if I have all faith, so as to move mountains, but do not have _____________, I am nothing.*
3 *And if I give all my possessions to feed the poor, and if I surrender my body to be burned, but do not have ___________, it profits me nothing.*

4 *Love is ______________, love is ______________ and is not ______________; love does not ____________ and is not _________________.*
5 *does not act _________________________; it does not seek its ____________, is not _____________________________, does not take into account a wrong suffered,*
6 *does not ________________ in unrighteousness, but rejoices with the ________________;*
7 *bears _________ things, believes __________ things, hopes ___________ things, endures __________ things.*
8 *Love never ______________;"*

13 *"but now faith, hope, love, abide these three; but the greatest of these is ______________."*

Look at the characteristics of love that you learned from the above verses. Which characteristics do you need to work on now, so that you will be ready to be a good wife or husband later? **(Circle any that apply.)**

Patience Kindness Not being jealous Not bragging Not being arrogant

Not acting unbecomingly (being mature) Not being selfish Not holding a grudge

Not rejoicing in sin Rejoicing with truth Bearing all things (perseverance and longsuffering)

Believing in others (trusts others) Hopeful Enduring Trustworthy

Who Should I Become?

Lesson 27

The righteousness of the blameless will smooth his way,
But the wicked will fall by his own wickedness.
Proverbs 11:5

Our last lesson gave us some good advice from the book of 1 Timothy about how to treat other young men and women. Titus also has some good advice about how we are to behave and what we need to be working at becoming.

Boys (and girls), look at Titus 2:6-8. These are character traits for young men to work on, but for young ladies not yet married, it is a good list to follow as well.

Verse 6: ***"Likewise urge the young men to be ___________________."***

What does it mean to be "sensible"? Being sensible is thinking before acting; measuring the consequences before making a choice. Not acting in anger, but rather in love. These verbs are in the form of "keep on being…" So this is not something that you decide to do, you do it one time, and you can check that one off! No, being sensible is an ongoing process of choosing the sensible thing time after time. The good news is that the more you make right choices the easier it gets!!

Verse 7-8: ***"…in all things show yourself to be an example of good deeds, with purity in doctrine, dignified, sound in speech which is beyond reproach, so that the opponent will be put to shame, having nothing bad to say about us."***

List the 4 character traits that a young man or woman should portray:

1.
2.
3.
4.

What might you do to be an example of good deeds? ______________________________
____

I believe that this is two-fold. We should set out to do good deeds, but we should also just be aware of opportunities that come up as we go along. For example, when I was a freshman in high school, I attended a Spanish class. One day a girl in class who was unpopular got sick and ran to the front of the room and threw up in the trash can. I quickly made my way to her side, picked up the trash can and led her out into the hall away from the eyes of the other classmates. I stayed with her until the teacher came out and sent me to go with her to the nurse. I reacted with a good deed when it was needed, because I was trying to be loving to my classmates. Other times I set out to do a good deed such as visiting someone who was sick or working in the clothes thrift store. Look around you. There are opportunities all around. Take these opportunities, but don't tell! I bet you will give yourself away from the big smile you wear all day, because it feels good to do good deeds for others!!

Then, young men (and women) are to be pure in doctrine. This is simply knowing what God's Word says about things like who Jesus is, who the Holy Spirit is, what the purpose of the church is, etc… **We learn doctrine by being intentional students of the word of God.** This includes reading, asking questions, listening, and praying.

Young people are supposed to be dignified. That doesn't mean you have to be stuffy and not have any fun, but it does mean that your fun is to be in good taste, not harming yourself or others, or making others feel uncomfortable. This is maturity. We tell our boys that being a teenager is a step towards adulthood rather than a choice to do what they want and to act like children and to get into trouble. If you don't see adults doing it, then you shouldn't do it either! For example, I dislike seeing teenagers at the mall or other public place kissing and hugging. Adults don't do that in public, so why should it be okay for kids to do it? **Be about growing up!!** The last lesson said to stay a kid, now I am saying to grow up. How does that work? Stay a kid in your activities and relationships until it is time to grow up, but be about growing mature in your spiritual walk with God and emotionally now.

The last suggestion is to be sound in speech. This includes not using cuss words or telling inappropriate jokes, but it is also more than that. It is being able to give an account of your words; being able to discuss different issues in a dignified manner without getting upset. It is being able to put ideas into logical thought patterns and to be able to present those thoughts to another in speech or writing. Notice that verse 8 says that we are to be sound in speech which is above reproach. We expect our boys to **be above reproach in all things**. That just means that they shouldn't do anything that would cause someone to question their integrity in word or deed.

If you make these principles the basis for your conduct, along with loving God, therefore loving God's people, then you will be on your way to maturity and adulthood!

Girls, add to this list the traits of Titus 2:5. **"…be sensible, pure, workers at home, being subject to their own husbands (dads for now), so the word of God will not be dishonored."**
(We will talk about being workers at home in a later lesson.)

Keep working on your memory verse.

Proverbs 21:23 - **"He who ___________ his ______________ and his ________________,**
Guards his ______________ from _________________."

And let endurance have its perfect result,
so that you may be perfect and complete,
lacking in nothing.
James 1:4

Explain what you think this statement means: "In marriage, ½ and ½ don't make a whole; rather a whole and a whole make a great marriage."

____

____

So what should you do to be whole? That starts now. If you procrastinate, it could be too late!!

Right now…

1. Work on your relationship with God – Bible reading, studying, and prayer.

2. Work on your relationship with your parents. Learning to respect them will teach you how to respect a spouse someday.

3. Work on talking out issues and disagreements with others. Be quick to forgive.

4. Work on responding to life with wisdom. Whatever life throws at you, think about how God would want you to react.

When that time comes to get married, you will be filled up, prayed up, lived up, and ready to go!!

When you squeeze a lemon, you get lemon juice. When you squeeze a sponge of water, you get water. What do people around you see when life squeezes you? Do you get angry, depressed, anxious, or joyful? ____

What characteristics do you want to ask God to begin to work on in your life? Circle any that apply.

honesty	forgiveness	encouragement	joyfulness	sweetness
loving	peacefulness	thankfulness	unselfishness	
not arguing	humility	being honest with emotions	perseverance	

Can you add any others?

____

Practical Proverbs Pp

Pray that God will help you to nurture these characteristics in your heart now, so that you will be ready when the love of your life steps into view.

A good way to gauge whether a person would make a good spouse or friend is how they treat their parents, especially the parent of the opposite sex. Does she respect her dad? Does he listen to his mom? How they treat their parents will be how they will tend to treat their spouse someday.

Your Body is Not Your Own

Lesson 28

**"Wine is a mocker and heavy drink a brawler,
And whoever is intoxicated by it is not wise."
Proverbs 20:1**

This lesson is going to talk about alcohol and drugs and sex outside of marriage, but these are only actions caused by a heart attitude. So we need to begin with the heart.

Read 1 Corinthians 3:16-17 and 1 Corinthians 6:19-20.

What do these verses say that our body is? ________________________

That's right the very temple of God!! The Holy Spirit is inside of you if you have asked Jesus to come into your life and be in control. He lives there. A temple is where a god lives and where a worshipper of that god can come and visit with that god. In the Old Testament the Israelites took great pride in the temple of God. It was overlaid with gold; it was ornate; it was the very center of their universe. When they prayed they prayed towards the temple. They revered the temple. It was in 72 A.D. when the temple in Jerusalem was burned down, that the nation of Israel dispersed or moved out of Jerusalem. Without the temple there was no reason to stay there. By this time, Jesus had died on the cross and a better plan was in place. God would no longer live in a building, but in the hearts of men. **Your body is the temple**. It should be revered. It should not be worshipped, but rather, God should be worshipped with your body.

What reason does 1 Corinthians 6:19-20 give for your body being a temple?

____

What was that price? ________________________________

Pretty costly, huh? Therefore, we are to glorify God in our body.

Romans 12:1 explains further what this means.

"Therefore I urge you, brethren, by the mercies of God, to present your bodies a living and holy sacrifice, acceptable to God which is your spiritual service of worship."

God cares what we do with our bodies!! Everything from eating well, getting enough sleep, and exercising, to not drinking, not doing drugs, **not** doing anything harmful to our body.

Practical Proverbs 

Let's look to the wisdom of Proverbs.

Read Proverbs 23:29-35.

List 6 effects that alcohol has on a person according to verse 29.
1.
2.
3.
4.
5.
6.

Verse 32 compares wine or alcohol to what? ________________________________

Notice the cycle that drinking leads to in verse 35 - this is alcoholism.

Now look at Proverbs 31:4-7.

Who shouldn't drink? ____

Who should drink? ____

Determine now in your heart that you won't take that first drink. You want to be a leader, maybe not a king, but a dad or mom, a CEO, a captain of a ship, etc... Don't let alcohol or drugs take those dreams from you.

Think for a minute of a raging river. How can you keep from being swept away by it? Stay away from it!! Never take that first step into the chaos! That should be your attitude about anything that will harm the body.

How is your memory verse coming along? Can you say it? Try and have it ready for the next lesson.

**Therefore I urge you, brethren,
by the mercies of God,
to present your bodies a living and holy sacrifice,
acceptable to God,
which is your spiritual service of worship.
Romans 12:1**

Next to each part of the body below, tell how you can use that member of the body to glorify God. Example: next to the feet, write feet can take the gospel to others. You may think of more than one per body part.

"Even so consider yourselves to be dead to sin, but alive to God in Christ Jesus. Therefore do not let sin reign in your mortal body so that you obey its lusts, and do not go on presenting the members of your body to sin as instruments of unrighteousness; but present yourselves to God as those alive from the dead, and your members as instruments of righteousness to God."

Romans 6:11-13

Modesty

Lesson 29

Your adornment must not be merely external –
braiding the hair, and wearing gold jewelry, or putting on dresses;
but let it be the hidden person of the heart…
a gentle and quiet spirit, which is precious in the sight of God.
1 Peter 3:3-4

Modesty can be a touchy subject because there are different opinions on what actions modesty should dictate and to what degree. In other words, my understanding of modesty may be to keep covered from the knee up and yours may be to keep covered from the ankle up. You will need to discuss with your parents what they approve of as modest. Our discussion will focus more on the heart issue. And, yes, boys, you, too, should dress and act modestly!!

Modesty comes from self-respect, respecting others, and respecting God. Usually the first thing we think about when we hear "modesty" is clothing. So let's start there. Modesty is wearing clothing that does not draw attention to yourself or your body. Wearing something that covers well, but glaringly yells out, "Hey, look at me!" is still immodest.

Read Jeremiah 9:23-24.

What are we not to boast about? ________________________________

What are we to boast about? ________________________________

Now read Philippians 3:3. What are the last 6 words of this verse? __________
____

When we are broadcasting our bodies in an immodest way we are boasting and putting confidence in the flesh. We want friends that like us for who we are inside, not for outward beauty. Proverbs 27:2 says, ***"Let another praise you and not your own mouth."***

God has called us to holiness. "Holy" means "set apart". We should be set apart from our world when our world is being immodest and indecent. A young girl can look nice without tight fitting or revealing clothes. A boy, in my opinion, just looks sloppy and undesirable, when the waistband of his pants are hanging halfway to his knees..

Your body is a special gift to give to your spouse on the night of your wedding. There is intrigue and desire where there are secrets. Keep your body a secret until it is the right time to reveal it.

Some very modest girls that I know throw all caution to the wind when it comes to swimming suits. But you can enjoy the water and friends without being immodest! At the end of this chapter are listed a couple of places where modest swimwear and clothing can be bought.

Girls think that they are attracting the looks and approval of young boys when they dress immodestly. God made boys to be visual. When a young girl walks by in revealing clothing, boys' thoughts go the way of impurity. Girls, don't be a hindrance to your brothers in Christ. Don't give them cause to sin.

Boys, you are human! You will have impure thoughts occasionally. But, sin begins when you dwell on those thoughts. Don't beat yourself up when you have an impure thought, confess it and think on something else.

> **Philippians 4:8 tells you where to turn your thoughts. What is true, honorable, right, pure, lovely, of good repute, excellent, and worthy of praise? ___________**

One of my sons decided that ice cream fit the bill!! But I think God was thinking of Himself and the Word of God! Memorize a verse or two and make it a habit to meditate on these verses when you are tempted by the sight of a girl.

Modesty can also be about how we behave. Unacceptable joking, lewd movements, crass words, flirtations, and even how you look at someone can be interpreted as immodest. Make sure your heart is right before God and that you are growing in holiness, that you look upon those of the opposite sex as a brother or a sister, and don't be the immodest one that would cause someone else to stumble.

Here is a link with a fashion show of modest clothing and a great song:
www.purefashion.com

Check these links out to purchase modest clothes:
www.4modesty.com
http://www.koshercasual.com/ModernlyModest

A good web site to find out what other teens and young adults think about modesty is:
www.therebelution.com/modestysurvey. This is a great site to discuss with your parents.

www.Swimmodest.com and www.modestsea.com have modest swimwear for girls.

I found several other conservative clothing lines online by googling "modest clothing".

Tell Proverbs 21:23 to a parent or an adult. Well done!

For those who are according to the flesh
set their minds on the things of the flesh,
but those who are according to the Spirit,
the things of the Spirit.
For the mind set on the flesh is death,
but the mind set on the Spirit is life and peace…
Romans 8:5-6

Modesty comes from a heart that is humble and knows how to respect the body. Let's see what God's Word says about our bodies.

Do you remember these two verses?
1 Corinthians 3:16-17
1 Corinthians 6:19-20

Your body is a ______________________ of the Holy Spirit.

Now look up 2 Corinthians 6:14-18. We are not to be bound together with unbelievers because, according to verse 16, the temple of God has no business being joined to ________________.

Unscramble these words to find out what other things we should stay away from because our body is God's temple.

1. hlcoalo (Proverbs 31:4-7 and 23:29-35) ______________________________
2. tsatoto (Leviticus 19:28) ______________________________
3. uyltgont (Proverbs 23:21) ______________________________
4. roamiyilmt (1 Corinthians 6:18) ______________________________
5. ins (Romans 6:12) ______________________________

Finally, look up Romans 12:1. Put these phrases in the right order according to this verse.

by the mercies of God   acceptable to God   which is your spiritual service

Therefore I urge you, brethren   a living and holy sacrifice   of worship

to present your bodies

____
____
____

Work

Lesson 30

He who tills his land will have plenty of food,
But he who follows empty pursuits will have poverty in plenty.
Proverbs 28:19

It is said that whatever we spend our time doing that is what we will become good at. What do you spend your time doing? Is it reading? Is it helping around the house? Cooking? Carpentry? Music? Video games? TV?

What do you spend most of your time doing? ______________________________

Right now, your work includes school work. Even though you have to do subjects you may not enjoy, the practice of studying and learning will pay off! You are exercising your mind so that it will be fit to learn the things that you will need for life.

We found a good example of someone using his time wisely when we went on a vacation in Albuquerque, New Mexico, and it rained the whole time we were there. We had to find things to do inside. We ran across an amazing museum there. It was called Tinkertown. "Over 40 years of carving and collecting have produced Ross J. Ward's Tinkertown. The folk art museum began with two main attractions: a carved wooden miniature three-ring circus that Ward created as a teenager, and a diminutive turn-of-the-century Western town he created in the 1960s. Today, those original animated displays are housed in a 22-room building, the walls of which are constructed with over 50,000 glass bottles. A variety of Ward's other collections are also on display — from wedding cake couples to Western memorabilia to a 35-foot antique sailboat." Ross Ward started as a young child carving wooden objects. Instead of sitting in front of the tv, he would carve. All of his carvings are in the museum and it is truly amazing!!

When I was a young Christian, I shared with an older lady in our church about my desire to write. She encouraged me to start journaling. I wrote about all the births of my kids, cute things they said and did, what my husband and I were doing, how I felt about each move we made, and what I thought about world events. I wrote about my thoughts on God's Word, sermons I heard, and conversations I had. I wrote for 25 years before I ever published anything! It was the same way with speaking. I entered my first speech contest in 6th grade and have spoken and taught Bible studies whenever I could. It was years before I started speaking for retreats and conferences. I still listen to other speakers to learn and grow. Now, I will admit that I was rarely if ever in the kitchen growing up and if I was I was making cookies! Now, as a wife and mother, I really struggle to be good at planning meals and putting something nutritious on the table three times a day!

Practical Proverbs 

God gave each one us different talents and desires. But He does have some advice about work for all of us. First of all, God assigned Adam work in the Garden of Eden **before** sin came into the world!

Read Genesis 2:15 and 2:19-20. What work was Adam to do?

1.
2.
3.

Work was not a part of the curse, it was part of God's perfect plan for man. We will be working in heaven as well! I know I won't be in the kitchen! I hope to be in the choir or doing landscaping!!

Next, God expects to have a certain attitude about work. **See Colossians 3:17 and 3:23.** He said it twice so it must be really important!

"Whatever you do in word or deed, do ________ in the name of the Lord Jesus, _________________ ________________ through Him to God the Father."

"Whatever you do, do your work _____________, as for the Lord rather than for men."

According to these verses, what should your attitude be towards work?

1.
2.

"Heartily" means with your whole heart and with gusto! Now, I admit, I don't like mopping floors. But, if I do them with an attitude of thanksgiving (We don't have dirt floors!) and with an attitude of praise because I had 5 healthy boys to make the mess, I can do the work heartily for Jesus!

What chore or task do you have that you need to have an attitude adjustment about?

____

Let God begin to change your heart as you attack you job with thanksgiving and gusto!

Our new memory verse is Proverbs 16:32. Read through it and get started!

The way of the lazy is as a hedge of thorns,
But the path of the upright is a highway.
Proverbs 15:19

Fill in the chart below.

	LAZY	**DILIGENT**
Proverbs 10:4	"Poor is he who works with a ____________________ hand,	But the hand of the diligent makes____________."
Proverbs 10:5	But he who sleeps in harvest is a son who acts ____________________________.	"He who gathers in harvest is a son who acts ____________________________,
Proverbs 10:26	"Like vinegar to the teeth and smoke to the eyes, So is the_____________ one to those who send him."	
Proverbs 12:24	But the _______________ hand will Be put to forced labor."	"The hand of the diligent will ___________________,
Proverbs 12:27	"A __________man does not roast His prey,	But the precious possession of a man is ________________."
Proverbs 13:4	"The soul of the sluggard (lazy) craves and gets __________________,	But the soul of the ___________is made fat."
Proverbs 14:23	But mere _________ leads only to poverty."	"In all labor there is profit,

Our Words

Lesson 31

**The mouth of the righteous flows with wisdom,
But the perverted tongue will be cut out.
Proverbs 10:31**

That sounds kind of drastic! When my oldest son was about seven years old, he read that verse and decided that he would never lie because *he* didn't want *his* tongue cut out! God is gracious and that is not a punishment we see today. But God does judge our words.

Read Matthew 12:36-37.

Jesus said, ***"But I tell you that every careless word that people speak, they shall give an accounting for it in the day of judgment. For by your words you will be ______________________ , and by your words you will be __________________."***

Words – spoken, written, or texted make up our conversations, our relationships, and our lives. A couple of verses earlier in Matthew, Jesus compares our words to two things.

Look at verses 33 and 35. What two things does he compare our words to?
1.
2.

He goes on to say in verse 34, ***"For the mouth speaks out of that which fills the heart."***

Read Proverbs 10:20 and see how the tongue of the righteous is compared to the heart of the wicked.

"The ______________________ of the righteous is as choice silver, The ____________ of the wicked is worth little."

So the key to godly speech is a godly heart!!

What are some of the sins of the mouth?

Look up these verses and list the sins that come out of our mouths (or fingers if we are texting.)

Proverbs 10:6 ____concealing violence___________

Proverbs 10:18 _____________________________ (there's two mentioned here.)

Proverbs 11:9 ______________________________

Proverbs 11:13 ______________________________

Proverbs 12:22 ______________________________

Proverbs 15:1 ______________________________

Proverbs 15:4 ______________________________

Proverbs 16:28 ______________________________ (There are two here.)

Proverbs 17:9 ______________________________ (what do we call that? ______________)

Proverbs 18:6 ______________________________

Proverbs 18:8 ______________________________

Proverbs 20:19 ______________________________ (There are two here.)

Proverbs 20:20 ______________________________

Proverbs 20:25 ______________________________

Proverbs 22:10 ______________________________ (There are four!)

Proverbs 24:28-29 ___________________________

Proverbs 25:14 ______________________________

Proverbs 25:23 ______________________________

Proverbs 25:24 ______________________________

Proverbs 26:28 ______________________________ (There are two here.)

Do you struggle with any of these sins of the mouth? **Write down the one that you need to pray for God to give you victory over.** ____

Give it to God and ask Him to help you.

Keep memorizing: ***"He who is slow to anger is better than the mighty,***
And he who rules his spirit, than he who captures a city."
Proverbs 16:32

Pleasant words are a honeycomb,
Sweet to the soul and healing to the bones.
Proverbs 16:24

Our words to others are so important. Fill in the blanks for Proverbs 18:21.

"______________ and ______________ are in the power of the tongue, And those who love it will eat its fruit."

How are death and life in the power of the tongue? You can speak words that encourage and build others up, or you can speak words that tear others down and discourage others. Solomon even says that a rightly placed word is "Like apples of gold in settings of silver." (Proverbs 25:11) I have never seen apples of gold in settings of silver, but I know that gold and silver are beautiful! So your words used well in the right circumstances are beautiful also!

Using your words well in right circumstances takes practice and discernment. But this can be learned!! This is not manipulation - make sure your heart is giving, not looking to receive.

Look for opportunities to give a word in a right circumstance and **record your successes below.**

1. Compliment someone for a job well done.

2. Compliment Mom on how pretty she looks.

3. Step in and turn a gossip session into a planning session.

4. Encourage a brother or sister or friend by letting them choose what to do.

5. Let Dad know how much you appreciate his hard work so that you can have nice clothes and food.

6. Tell a teacher or coach thank you for taking the time to teach you.

7. Encourage someone who is discouraged.

Remember to use your words to give life to others!!

Lying

Lesson 32

A false witness will perish,
But the man who listens to the truth will speak forever.
Proverbs 21:28

Stretching the truth, telling a half-truth, a white lie, a fib, a whopper, just an exaggeration, flattery, a falsehood – when you come right down to it, they are all lies.

At our house, **a half-truth is a whole lie**. That means that you don't leave anything out, and everything that you tell is truth.

Why does God care if we lie or not? Is it really *that* big of a deal?

Remember, our God is holy, pure, and righteous. He wants His children to also be holy, pure, and righteous. We are being "sanctified" in Christ. Sanctified means that we are growing mature, complete, closer to perfection. That growth can't happen if there is any sin in our lives. God does not grade sins from small to large sins. **All sins separate us from God**. Jesus died on the cross for *all* our sins – from white lies to murder. A liar needs God's saving grace as much as a murderer! After becoming a Christian, those lies can keep you from growing and having a relationship with God.

John 14:6 says that Jesus is ***"…the way, the truth, and the life."*** If we want to be like Jesus, then we must walk in truth in all things, being above reproach.

Why do we lie anyway? The top two reasons are to protect someone or ourselves from punishment and to not disappoint someone. If we understand that punishment is a positive influence in our lives to make us more like Jesus, that it is given in love, and that our worth is not based on our performance, then these two excuses don't work.

Choose truth. You remember the old saying: **What a tangled web we weave,**
When we practice to deceive.

This is true, because when you tell a lie then you tend to have to tell another and another to keep from being caught in the first lie. Then you begin to forget what you told to whom and it becomes a real mess. There is no peace until you confess to God and the one you lied to. Confession is not easy, but its reward is peace and renewed relationship with God and man.

Let's look up a couple of verses about lying.

Proverbs 14:25 ***"A truthful witness saves lives, but he who utters lies is ________________."***

Practical Proverbs

Proverbs 19:9 ***"A false witness will not go ____________________, And he who tells lies will ____________________."***

Proverbs 20:17 ***"Bread obtained by falsehood is sweet to a man, But afterwards his mouth will be filled with ________________________."***

This truth is evident when you lie and it seems like you got away with it, but then your life is complicated by having to keep lying. One year I accidently saw a Christmas gift in a closet before it was wrapped and placed under the tree. It was a magic set and I was so excited. My mom saw that the closet door was open and asked me if I had gotten into the closet. I lied because I didn't want to spoil her surprise (disappoint her). When Christmas morning came and I opened the magic set, I had to lie again and act surprised. There was no joy in receiving that gift. My joy had been turned into guilt.

Proverbs 21:6 ***"The acquisition of treasures by a lying tongue is a fleeting vapor, the pursuit of ________________________."***

I found this out when I was about 12 years old and helped my sister shoplift a heart shaped box filled with candy. I was not a Christian, but I knew better! We hid the candy and ate it when we could in private. It never tasted very good – and I am talking about chocolate here! We got caught and had to go to the store and confess. Boy, was that humbling! I never, ever, stole anything ever again!!

Proverbs 21:28 ***"A false witness will ______________________, but the man who listens to the truth will speak ______________________."***

Proverbs 25:18 ***"Like a ______________ and a _____________________ and a sharp _____________ is a man who bears false witness against his neighbor."***

Be ready to say your memory verse after two more lessons!

"He who is ______________ to _____________ is better than the __________ , And he who ___________ his _____________, than he who _______________ a city." Proverbs 16:32

A false witness will not go unpunished,
And he who tells lies will not escape.
Proverbs 19:5

Write about a time that you lied, what you learned, and any decisions you made about lying at that time.

Judging Others

Lesson 33

Do not reprove a scoffer or he will hate you,
Reprove a wise man and he will love you.
Proverbs 9:8

How do you know if someone is a scoffer or a wise man? Many Christians are under the false belief that they are not to judge others. We will look at what the Bible has to say about this today.

First, there is a warning for us. 1 Corinthians 4:6 says, ***"…so that you may learn not to exceed what is written, so that no one of you will become arrogant in behalf of one against the other."***

This verse is saying that we should not judge others beyond what the Word of God says. So it is important that we know what the Bible says about judging.

Let's look first at whom we are to judge and why, then we will look at whom and what we are not to judge. Lastly, we will look at what our attitude should be when we judge.

According to Matthew 7:15, who are we to judge? ________________________________

A false prophet is someone either outside of the church congregation or within the church congregation that is speaking lies about God's Word. They look good, seem to speak truth to those who do not know God's Word, and often use God's Word for personal gain. We are to judge these prophets by their fruits – their outward actions and the consequences of their teachings. Remember, first of all that God is always 100% right. If a prophet seems right part of the time, that is not good enough! Cult leaders are obviously false prophets, but there are those within the established church as well. How do we know the true prophets/preachers from the false ones? **Read 1 John 4:1-2.**

> ***"Beloved, do not believe every spirit, but test the spirits to see whether they are from God, because many false prophets have gone out into the world. By this you know the Spirit of God: every spirit that confesses that Jesus Christ has come in the flesh is from God; and every spirit that does not confess Jesus is not from God…"***

What test should we use to determine falsehood from truth? The Truth – Jesus Christ. The teachings of every true pastor/prophet will stand against the truth of the Word of God. That is why knowing your Bible is so important!! Most new members of cults come from a mainstream protestant denomination. They were lured in with just enough truth to make the cult leader's claims seem to be true. But because they didn't know the whole counsel of the word of God, they were open to falsehood.

Bill Gothard, a preacher/teacher gives this illustration. When a bank hires a new teller, they want them to be able to tell the difference between a real dollar bill and a fake one. They do **not** give them forgeries to study. They give them the real deal only. They finger them, spread them out, touch them over and over, etc... until they can feel what the real bill feels like. Then, if a forged bill comes into their hands they recognize it immediately, because they know that it is not like the true ones!! That is the way that we should be with truth. We should know it so well, that when falsehood comes into our lives, we can pick it out quickly! We should judge false prophets so that they cannot influence the church and turn them from Christ!

Another type of person that we should judge, (and this will come as a shock for some of you) is another believer that is choosing to sin. **Read 1 Corinthians 5:1-5**. Here you see the Apostle Paul judging the sin within the church. We should judge other believers so that we might point them towards being restored in Jesus. **Read James 5:19-20**. This is again, within the body of believers.

But there are times when our judgment is not right and Biblical. **Look up the following verses and write down what they say about judging.**

Matthew 7:1 ____

Luke 6:37 ____

Romans 14:10 ____

Romans 14:13 ____

1 Corinthians 5:12 ____

The key is really very simple. We are to judge believers when their actions are sin – when their actions are explicitly against the Word of God. We are not to judge things that are not essential to salvation and walk of faith – things like what someone wears, what they eat, how they celebrate a holiday, which version of the Bible they use, etc. ..

Let's look at a couple more verses about this and then we will look at the attitude that we must have if we are to be in a position to judge others that they might be restored to Christ.

Read 1 Corinthians 6:12 and 10:23. What is lawful for the believer ______________

____

But are these things always the best? ______________

Again, there is a key to this! **Read 1 Corinthians 10:31. Write the last 7 words here**:

____

Practical Proverbs 

Now, turn to Romans chapter 14. Read verses 1-10. This will put things into perspective for you. Judge a believer who is living in sin, but do not judge them for non-essential things. God loves each of us as a unique child. What is best for one, may not be best for another. God does not give us all the same experiences because we are not all the same!!

If we see a brother or sister in Christ sinning, how should we approach them? Let's start off with 2 Corinthians 3:5, James 4:10, and 1 Corinthians 4:6-7. What one word could you use to sum up these verses? ________________________

I hope you wrote humility! We need to go to one another with a great sense of who our God is, and knowing that we, too, were sinners and can still choose to sin. We are to go to restore the other, not to condemn him/her. We are to go with love. If they continue in sin, then there should be a consequence. 1 Timothy 5:20 says, ***"Those who continue in sin, rebuke in the presence of all, so that the rest also will be fearful of sinning."***

Humility also includes taking an assessment of our own relationship with God, before we go to a brother or sister. This is what Matthew 7:1-5 says. Notice verse 5 says, ***"...first take the log out of your own eye, and then you will see clearly to take the speck out of your brother's eye."***

Galatians 6:4 reminds us to ***"...examine [our] own work..."*** and 2 Corinthians 13:5 says to ***"Test yourselves to see if you are in the faith; examine youselves!"***

Lastly, remember that God is sovereign and He holds the right to judge. Read **Romans 14:10-12.** Who should you be most concerned with? ________________

Be ready to say Proverbs 16:32 after the next lesson.

...for He is coming to judge the earth;
He will judge the world with righteousness
And the peoples with equity.
Psalm 98:9

Often we judge because we don't know the whole story.

How would you judge the following scenarios? Circle guilty or innocent for each one. Then read the rest of the story found on the next page.

1. John was told to be home on time. He is 10 minutes late. Guilty or innocent?

2. Henry came home with the first place trophy in baseball even though he was accused of cheating. You find a bat with cork in it in his garage. Guilty or innocent?

3. You walk in the living room and see that there is dog poop on your mom's favorite chair. Pookie Dog is sitting in the corner. Guilty or innocent?

4. Darlene gets the lead in the school play. Her mom is the drama teacher. She must have played favorites. Guilty or innocent?

5. Brad got in trouble last year for shop lifting. You see him at the mall with a "bump" under his jacket. Guilty or innocent?

6. Nellie lost her favorite jacket. Brenda comes to church on Sunday with a jacket just like Nellie's. Guilty or innocent?

7. Dad's hammer was left out in the rain and it rusted. Your little brother was the last one that you saw using it. Guilty or innocent?

8. You drove by a night club and saw your pastor there. Guilty or innocent?

9. Your grandma said that she sent you a check for your birthday. You never got it. Mom just got a new dress. Guilty or innocent?

10. A member of your church was arrested for hurting his wife. She comes to church with bruises. Guilty or innocent?

The Rest of the Story

1. John was riding with a friend. The friend needed to talk to someone at the church before he could leave.

2. Henry's dad is a coach and made a cork bat to show his players what one looked like so that they would never use one in a game.

3. Your dad brought home a new puppy and the puppy messed on the chair. Pookie Dog is hiding from the new puppy.

4. Darlene is a talented actress and often gets the lead roles in plays.

5. The "bump" is really his mother's purse. She left it in the car and sent him to go get it. He didn't want anyone to see him carrying a purse so he slipped it under his jacket.

6. Target had a great sale on that jacket at the end of last season. They both bought one.

7. Your mom used it to hang a picture and stuck it in a pile that she was taking to the garage. It fell out on the way and she didn't notice it.

8. Your pastor got a call that his sister was at the night club and needed help. He went to get her.

9. Your Grandma wrote the check, but never mailed it. Mom's new dress was bought with *her* birthday money.

10. The wife had fallen out of the deer stand while helping her husband make sure everything was ready for deer season. Her jealous sister called the police and said that her husband had hit her.

As you can see, even though the circumstances looked a little bit weird, everyone was innocent!! Be careful to have all the information when deciding to judge a situation. And be extra careful not to spread untrue rumors!!

Suffering

Lesson 34

Do not boast about tomorrow,
For you do not know what a day may bring forth.
Proverbs 27:1

One of the biggest questions that non-Christians have that may keep them from becoming Christians is, "How can a loving God allow such suffering in this world?" Theologians have written about and discussed this question for years. Simply put, suffering is a result of Satan's rule on earth, man's sinful nature, and consequences to our own choices.

Sometimes we suffer just because we live in a world controlled by Satan. When Adam and Eve sinned in the garden God allowed Satan to take over authority of this world.

> Ephesians 2:1-2 says, ***"And you were dead in your trespasses and sins, in which you formerly walked according to the course of this world, according to the prince of the ____________ ______ ______ ________, of the spirit that is now working in the sons of disobedience…"***

That's Satan. And God has allowed him power over earth for this time. I always say that if you live in a garbage pit, you will get garbage on you. If you live in this world where Satan reigns, you will get touched by his evil or the consequences of his evil – sickness, death, discouragement, disease, famine, tornadoes, earthquakes, etc...

When Adam sinned, he lost the ability to have a relationship with God. He now had a sin nature that was passed on to every descendant of Adam – every human being. Suffering often comes because of this sin nature – greed, lust, anger, etc… Often people are victims of others' sinful choices. A child beaten by her father is a victim of her father's sin.

Sometimes, though, suffering is a direct consequence of our choices. When we sin or make foolish decisions, suffering can occur. One of my sons decided that he wanted to bull ride in rodeos. We talked about the possible consequences, and he decided to go ahead and ride. After two trips to the emergency room, one by helicopter, he realized that this decision was not taking him in the direction that he wanted to go. He is still recovering from a torn ligament in the knee, a broken facial bone, and bruised ribs. He will most likely suffer pain from these injuries for the rest of his life. These injuries have definitely caused him pain now! And they have kept him from participating in things that he wanted to do. This suffering is a direct result of his choices.

God allows His people to suffer because of their own sinful choices, because of others' sin, and because of Satan's rule, but also because we need to grow closer to God. If we are not challenged by this world, we will not lean on God who is there for us - by leaning on God we learn to trust, to love, and to rest. **Suffering is an opportunity to be near to God!!** Jesus did make us a promise:

> **Hebrews 13:5** ***"Make sure that your character is free form the love of ______________, being content with what you have; for He Himself has said, 'I will never ________________ you, nor will I ever ____________________ you."***

Jesus will always be here with us through anything that this world can throw at us!!

Jesus promises that we will not go through our suffering alone. He will be with us and give us the grace and courage and strength to go through it.

Suffering reminds us of our need for a Savior. It is in a time of great suffering, that our faith grows. My two heroes of the faith are Joni Eareckson-Tada and Corrie Ten Boom. Joni was paralyzed from the neck down when she dove into a lake at age 17. She is now in her 50's and she was asked if she would change her life if she could. She replied that she would not change anything, because her accident and handicap led her to a deeper relationship with God. Corrie Ten Boom was Danish and hid Jewish refugees in her home during WWII. She was caught and sent to a concentration camp. There she saw thousands of people die including her sister. When she was released, she began to tell her story of God's faithfulness, even in those terrible circumstances. She grew close to God and learned that in all suffering, God is there. These two courageous women could agree with **Romans 8:18:**

> **"For I consider that the sufferings of this present time are not worthy to be compared with the glory that is to be revealed to us."**

Suffering is only for a time, eternity and our relationship with God are forever!

Jesus suffered on the cross. He did not deserve the pain and agony of the cross or the emotional pain of our sins and separation from the Father, but he looked beyond the cross to the joy of being with the Father for eternity and with being able to share that eternity with us! (Hebrews 12:2). We can also look to the joy of an eternity free from pain and full of the love and peace of Jesus!

Know this: suffering is never a good excuse for sin! 1 Peter 4:19 says, ***"Therefore, those also who suffer according to the will of God shall entrust their souls to a faithful Creator in doing what is right."***

It is tempting to become selfish, angry, grumpy, or prideful when we suffer. But suffering is common to all men. As Christians we need to allow our suffering to lead us to God. I was born with a form of spina bifida that allowed me to walk and even to play softball, but I have had a lot of pain since birth. I was told that I should never have been able to stand, let alone

walk, or have children. Now that I am getting older and have had several surgeries, I am losing my mobility and the pain gets worse. I can choose to be angry and grumpy, but I choose instead to be thankful for the ability to walk, and I choose to enjoy my boys doing the things that I *can* do. We took the family to Enchanted Rock State Park in Texas today. The boys ran and climbed and explored. My husband and I walked to the bottom of the rock, looked up and enjoyed God's creation; then we sat at a picnic table and played board games. I chose to praise the Lord because I could enjoy the sun and hear about the boys' exploits rather than sit and complain because I could not go with them.

Suffering comes with being a part of the human race. Your attitude in the suffering is your choice – you can wallow in it or grow from it.

Say Proverbs 16:32 to a parent or an adult.

After you have suffered for a little while,
the God of all grace,
who called you to His eternal glory in Christ,
will Himself perfect, confirm, strengthen and establish you.
1 Peter 5:10

Suffering will come. It is part of being human. How will you handle it?

Read this parable and share it with your family.

A young woman went to her mother and told her about her life and how things were so hard for her. She did not know how she was going to make it and wanted to give up. She was tired of fighting and struggling. It seemed as one problem was solved, a new one arose.

Her mother took her to the kitchen. She filled three pots with water and placed each on a high fire. Soon the pots came to boil. In the first she placed carrots, in the second she placed eggs, and in the last she placed ground coffee beans. She let them sit and boil, without saying a word.

In about twenty minutes she turned off the burners. She fished the carrots out and placed them in a bowl. She pulled the eggs out and placed them in a bowl. Then she ladled the coffee out and placed it in a bowl.

Turning to her daughter, she asked, "Tell me what you see."

"Carrots, eggs, and coffee," she replied.

Her mother brought her closer and asked her to feel the carrots. She did and noted that they were soft. The mother then asked the daughter to take an egg and break it. After pulling off the shell, she observed the hard-boiled egg. Finally, the mother asked the daughter to sip the coffee. The daughter smiled as she tasted its richness and savored its aroma.

The daughter then asked, "What does it mean, mother?"

Her mother explained that each of these objects had faced the same adversity – boiling water. Each reacted differently.

The carrot went in strong, hard, and unrelenting. However, after being subjected to the boiling water, it softened and became weak. The egg had been fragile. Its thin outer shell had protected its liquid interior, but after sitting through the boiling water, its inside became hardened. The ground coffee beans were unique, however. After they were in the boiling water, they had changed the water.

"Which are you?" she asked her daughter. "When adversity knocks on your door, how do you respond? Are you a carrot, an egg or a coffee bean?"

Suffering is not a choice, life happens. How you choose to react to life is up to you!

Virtuous Woman

Lesson 35
(Boys do this lesson also)

An excellent wife, who can find?
For her worth is far above jewels.
Proverbs 31:10

Chapter 31 of Proverbs is probably the most quoted and studied chapter of Proverbs. It tells of a woman's role in the home. The home is the foundation for each person in it – husband, wife, and kids. And **it is the woman's responsibility to set the tone.** The old saying goes "If Mama ain't happy, ain't nobody happy!" Boys, you can look at these verses and know what to look for in someone that you might want for a wife someday. So, let's get started.

Read verses 10-12 and 23.

This is how a godly woman relates to her husband. **TRUST** is the big word here. Gossiping or telling others about private matters will break that trust. When there is trust in a marriage, there is peace and confidence. That allows the man to be about other things such as providing for and protecting the family. A godly woman's heart seeks to do good to her husband. He is to be first priority!! This can be hard after kids come along, but it is essential. The most important relationship for any child is not his/her relationship to Mom or his/her relationship to Dad, rather it is the relationship between Mom and Dad. When kids see that Mom and Dad love each other and work together, then they feel secure and loved. Boys, then, must grow up to be trustworthy; doing what is right and good so their wives can trust and rest in their husbands' protection and provision.

Read verses 13-16, 24.

This godly woman is a business woman!! While home should be the priority, especially when there are children in the home, women may have other pursuits. The Proverbs 31 woman's pursuits center around providing clothing and food for her family. This does not take us as much time as it used to because of all the time saving inventions like the dishwasher, sewing machine, etc... **However, the raising of godly children and a clean an orderly home should be the top priority.** Your family should never be ashamed to be seen in public nor should they be hungry. This does *not* mean that every child should have the latest fashions and coolest stuff.

I have found that the best way to be able to make my home the priority is to do jobs *from* home that allow me enough time to cook, clean, teach, train, and do laundry. For me that has included teaching piano lessons, making gift baskets, decorating cakes, babysitting, and writing. Friends of mine are nurses and work the weekend or evening shifts at the hospital when their husbands can be home to care for the children. This requires a lot of cooperation, but there are ways for a woman to work outside of the home and not neglect the family.

Girls, what might you prepare yourself to do from the home that will bring in some extra cash, but not take away from raising your children?

____

____

Read verse 17

This godly woman is fit!! She takes care of her body. She exercises! This gives her energy to get through each day with joy. (Boys need to stay fit so that they can provide for and protect their families.)

What kind of exercise do you like to do? ____________________________

If you are not exercising regularly, there is no better time than now to begin!

Read verses 18–22, 27.

This is not a lazy woman!! You may be a morning person or you may be a night owl. Either one is fine just make sure that you are not wasting the time that God has given you. Learn a new skill – cooking, baking, sewing, knitting, crochet, embroidery, painting, woodwork, gardening, etc... The list is endless and will serve you well in the days to come. The Proverbs 31 woman also has enough time and food left over to help take care of the poor. All her efforts were not for her immediate family, but once that responsibility was met, she was able to help others. You can begin to do that now! You could volunteer at church or at a local pregnancy center or food line or shelter. (Boys, you are also needed as volunteers and you can gain good work skills through volunteering.)

What can you do to volunteer? ____________________________________

Read verses 25–26.

What 5 characteristics does the godly woman have in these verses?

1.
2.
3.
4.
5.

When a woman is right with God, right with her husband, and makes her children and her home a priority, she will be at peace. This is also true for you now. When God is the center of your world, you are obeying your parents, choosing good friends, and making wise choices, you will be at peace.

Practical Proverbs

Read verses 28–31.

Even though praise is not our motivation to do well, it is a nice side effect of a job well done! Do your best!! I had a young woman ask me how she could do it all – the house, the kids, the husband, teaching, and still have time for herself. Here's my answer:

> **First**, it is important to have some time for God because that will fill you up and give you the strength for the rest of the tasks. Then find time for you. We live in a fast paced, high tech world. It is easy to be too busy from morning until too late at night. Put down your phone and computer for a time each day and draw, or dance, or shoot baskets, or read a book. This time by yourself will give you energy to be with others and to get your tasks done.
>
> **Secondly**, prioritize! You can begin learning to prioritize your days now. What has to be done? What needs to be done? What things would you like to get done but could be put off until tomorrow? What things need to wait for another day? Don't get stressed because you have too much to do – prioritize and then do the next thing next. Let your list help you, not rule over you! What you don't get done today, can be moved to tomorrow's list.

How do you eat an elephant? One bite at a time!! That's also how we get it all done. And we do it with joy!!

A good perspective on the Proverbs 31 woman is that this is an older woman looking back at all the phases of her life. When you look back, you want to feel confident that you did your best for yourself, your mate, your children, and your God! Will God say to you, ***"Well done, My good and faithful servant"? (Matthew 25:23)***

We have finished all your memory verses! Be ready to say them after your next lesson!

Review them!!
The definition of wisdom
Proverbs 3:5-6
Psalm 1:1-3
Proverbs 14:12
Proverbs 4:23
Proverbs 21:23
Proverbs 16:32

**Nevertheless, each individual among you also
is to love his own wife even as himself,
and the wife must see to it that she respects her husband.**
Ephesians 5:33

A GODLY PERSON

Word Bank:

Confident	Diligent	FearsGod	Praiseworthy
Creative	Generous	Strong	Trustworthy
Untiring	Dignified	Excellent	Doesgooddeeds
Kind	Teacher	Wise	

B	T	I	T	R	U	S	T	W	O	R	T	H	Y	D
D	E	X	F	C	Q	R	D	J	I	F	O	D	G	E
C	A	A	L	I	Z	F	O	P	M	S	K	I	A	Y
O	C	F	N	N	K	A	E	Q	U	P	E	G	L	H
N	H	O	R	M	C	Z	S	S	T	R	O	N	G	Y
F	E	G	T	O	M	B	G	L	Y	A	U	I	N	S
I	R	X	K	C	H	E	O	J	U	I	D	F	I	C
D	A	F	C	R	N	C	O	E	L	S	X	I	R	D
E	Z	K	Q	E	G	X	D	R	P	E	W	E	I	I
N	I	V	R	A	L	U	D	R	A	W	R	D	T	L
T	R	O	V	T	A	L	E	Y	M	O	V	X	N	I
C	U	L	K	I	N	D	E	C	H	R	B	T	U	G
S	K	P	U	V	R	Y	D	N	Z	T	B	J	U	E
H	W	D	C	E	K	L	S	I	T	H	R	N	W	N
F	E	A	R	S	G	O	D	C	B	Y	A	K	C	T

Truth

Lesson 36

Buy truth, and do not sell it,
Get wisdom and instruction and understanding.
Proverbs 23:23

Truth. The world will tell you that truth changes. That each of us have our own truth. That each circumstance requires a different truth. That we can define our own truth.

God's Word says that **Jesus is the Truth** (John 14:6). You will set your life course by your beliefs. You must decide what you believe, not because Mom and Dad have told you to believe this or that, but because you have determined in your heart by the reading of God's Word what is true.

It is said that you are as sick as your sickest secret. 1 John says that, ***"No lie is of the truth."*** When you reveal that secret to the light and apply truth to it, it can no longer hold any power over you. Write out John 8:32.

____

____

What will you be free from? From the bondage of lies, the rejection of God, the judgment of God, and from self-condemnation. You may still have to suffer some of the consequences of your sin, though. Someone who steals and is sent to jail may become a Christian while in jail. He will experience the freedom from guilt and the peace of God, but he will still have to finish his jail sentence.

Jesus prayed to the Father for future believers (you and me) and asked that God would ***"...sanctify them in the truth; Your word is truth."*** (John 17:17).

The Holy Spirit is called the Spirit of Truth.

Read John 16:13.

According to this verse what will the Spirit of Truth guide you into? __________

____

And that journey is called life. If you abide in God and in His Word, the Spirit will reveal truth to you all along the way - truth about your circumstances, truth about others, truth about yourself, and truth about God. **And it will never change!** Truth is absolute - all the time, for all people, for every circumstance.

David had a lot to say about truth in the Psalms. Fill in the blanks for these verses.

Psalm 25:5 ***"Lead me in Your truth and teach me,***
For You are the _____________ of my _____________________;
For You I wait all the day."

Psalm 25:10 ***"All the paths of the Lord are lovingkindness and truth***
To those who _____________ His covenant and His testimonies."

Psalm 26:3 ***"For Your lovingkindness is before my eyes,***
And I have ___________________ in Your truth."

Psalm 16:7-9 ***"I will bless the Lord who has _________________________ me;***
Indeed, my mind instruct me in the night.
I have set the Lord continually before me;
Because He is at my right hand, I will not be shaken.
Therefore my heart is glad and my glory rejoices;
My flesh also will dwell securely."

And the counsel of the Lord is Truth!!

Psalm 86:11 ***"Teach me Your way, O Lord, I will walk in Your ______________;***
Unite my heart to fear Your name."

In all of these verses we find that where God is there is truth. If we want to experience truth, we must experience God.

Even if you don't like math, there is certainty to it. How much is 4 + 4? 4 + 4 is **always** 8, never 5 or 6 or 7 or 9. You can know if you are right or wrong with confidence. Other subjects such as English are not so precise and actually change. I learned and taught my children to put a comma between each item of a list and before the word "and". Now the new teaching is to leave the comma out before the "and". English composition and grammar is subjective. (Subject to someone's opinion - what I think is a great paper, your teacher may hate.) Math is objective. It is the way it is for everyone, in every situation. **Truth is objective – it never changes and is the same for everyone.**

Truth is simply a statement of what really is. When Moses stood before the burning bush, God told Moses His name – "I AM". That is the ultimate truth. **Our God was and is and ever more will be. He encompasses everything and every time and all eternity. He is the Alpha and Omega – the Beginning and the End (and everything in between).**

I once saw a bumper sticker that read, **"Know God, know truth. No God, no truth."**

Say all of your memorized Bible verses to a parent.

If you continue in My word,
then you are truly disciples of Mine;
and you will know the truth,
and the truth will make you free.
John 8:31-32

What are the basic truths that you believe? Look at each verse below and write out the truth that it reveals.

Genesis 1:1 ______________________________

____

Romans 5:8 ______________________________

____

Romans 10:9-10 ______________________________

____

Romans 8:1 ______________________________

____

Romans 8:15-17 ______________________________

____

1 Peter 3:12 ______________________________

____

1 Peter 5:7 ______________________________

____

2 Timothy 1:7 ______________________________

____

Colossians 2:13-14 ______________________________

____

Colossians 2:2-3 ______________________________

____

Philippians 1:6 ______________________________

____

Philippians 3:10-11 ______________________________

____

What a mighty God we serve!! Let praises be forever on your lips and His name always in your heart.

I leave you with this: 1 Thessalonians 5:23-24:

> **"Now may the God of peace Himself sanctify you entirely; and may your spirit and soul and body be preserved complete, without blame at the coming of our Lord Jesus Christ. Faithful is He who calls you, and He also will bring it to pass."**

Appendix A

Recommended Reading:

Any biography is good with proper discussion. We can learn from the twisted mind of Hitler and the unfaithfulness of Benedict Arnold as well as the godly attitudes and lives of Billy Graham and Joni Eareckson-Tada. Three excellent series of **Christian biographies** are:

The Sower Series (Mott Media)
Christian Heroes: Then and Now (YWAM)
Heroes of the Faith (Barbour Books)

Other Great Books:

Eareckson-Tada, Joni, Joni: An Unforgettable Story, (Zondervan, 2001).

Elliott, Elisabeth, Through Gates of Splendor, (Tyndale House Publishers, Inc., 1981).

Hale, Mabel, revised by Karen Andreola, Beautiful Girlhood, (Great Expectations Book Co., 1993).

Hurnard, Hannah, Hinds' Feet on High Places, (Tyndale House Publishers, Inc., 1977).

Johnson, Kevin and Josh McDowell, God's Will, God's Best for Your Life, (Bethany House, 2000).

Malley, Sarah and Harold, Making Brothers and Sisters Best Friends, (Tomorrow's Forefathers, 2004).

Malley, Sarah, Before You Meet Prince Charming, (Tomorrow's Forefathers, 2007).

Marshall, Peter and David Manuel, The Light and the Glory, (Fleming H. Revell,1977).

McGee, Dr. Robert, The Search For Significance, (Thomas Nelson, 2003).

Muller, George, The Autobiography of George Muller, (Whitaker House, ,

Munger, Robert, My Heart, Christ's Home, (Intervarsity Press, 2001).

Olson, Bruce, Bruchko, (Charisma House, 1995).

Sheldon, Charles M., In His Steps, (Barbour Publishing, Inc.,1985).

Ten Boom, Corrie and John Sherrill, The Hiding Place, (Mass Market Paperback, 2006).

White, JB, Tiger and Tom and Other Stories for Boys, (A.B. Publishing, 1993).

White, JB, The King's Daughter and Other Stories for Girls, (A. B. Publishing, 1993).